AF413146

THE NUMEROLOGY ANSWER BOOK

105 Questions & their Answers

INDIA · SINGAPORE · MALAYSIA

THE NUMEROLOGY ANSWER BOOK

105 Questions & their Answers

PRIYANKA KUUMAR

Copyright © Priyanka Kuumar 2024
All Rights Reserved.

ISBN
Paperback 979-8-89556-976-4
Hardcase 979-8-89588-255-9

This book has been published with all efforts taken to make the material error-free after the consent of the author. However, the author and the publisher do not assume and hereby disclaim any liability to any party for any loss, damage, or disruption caused by errors or omissions, whether such errors or omissions result from negligence, accident, or any other cause.

While every effort has been made to avoid any mistake or omission, this publication is being sold on the condition and understanding that neither the author nor the publishers or printers would be liable in any manner to any person by reason of any mistake or omission in this publication or for any action taken or omitted to be taken or advice rendered or accepted on the basis of this work. For any defect in printing or binding the publishers will be liable only to replace the defective copy by another copy of this work then available.

PROLOGUE

How did my fascination with Numerology begin?

When I was merely 13 or 14 years old, my family embarked on a vacation to Madras- now known as Chennai. However, our plans took an unexpected turn when my mother fell ill, necessitating an extended stay. In close proximity to our hotel, there was a bustling market. To alleviate our boredom, my father took me and my younger brother there to indulge in a little shopping. It was during this time that I encountered a Numerology book by Cheiro, titled "Ankon Mein Chupa Bhavishya." Without any prior knowledge of Numerology, I made an impulsive decision to purchase the book. Little did I know that this serendipitous encounter would ignite a profound fascination within me. Some might call it love at first sight, and perhaps, it was.

From that moment on, I delved deeper into the subject, acquiring more books such as Linda Goodman's "Sun Signs" and "Moon Signs." Time swiftly passed, and the journey of my life led me through various paths, which included becoming a fashion designer, jewellery designer, fashion teacher, writer, personal development trainer, motivational speaker, counsellor, and eventually, a Numerologist. If you are familiar with the characteristics associated with numbers, you may have deduced that I am a number 3 person. Spot on!

The motivation behind writing this book was to address the numerous queries I often receive about Numerology, its workings, benefits, and more. While I hold a deep love for my chosen field, I do find it disheartening when people approach me haphazardly, seeking insights into their future without truly understanding the subject. This has prompted me to pen this book, presenting a collection of questions and answers aimed at dispelling doubts and misconceptions about Numerology. It is my sincere desire to make Numerology accessible and enlightening for all who seek its wisdom.

Numerology, a vast and multifaceted subject, unveils countless layers and dimensions for exploration. Its intricate web of knowledge invites seekers from all walks of life to indulge their inquisitive minds in unravelling the mysteries that surround us. While individual interests may vary, the allure of numerology transcends personal inclinations, captivating anyone with a yearning to understand the profound "whys" that underpin existence itself.

In this endeavour, I have diligently curated a collection of 105 diverse and thought-provoking questions, aiming to provide a panoramic view of this captivating subject. Through this array of inquiries, I aspire to offer you a glimpse into the expansive landscape of numerology, an intellectual playground where knowledge-seekers can satiate their thirst for understanding.

Remember, numerology is not confined to a select few; it embraces all who dare to explore its intricacies. It serves as a gateway to unravel the enigmatic forces that shape our lives, shedding light on the deeper meanings embedded within our numerical fabric.

So, whether you find yourself drawn to numerology's mystical allure, or simply possess an innate curiosity about the world around you- this compilation stands as a testament to the inclusivity of numerology's appeal. Its purpose is to beckon all inquisitive minds and ignite a passion for unravelling the intricate tapestry of numbers.

Join me on this extraordinary journey as we embark on a quest to unveil the secrets of numerology. Let us delve into its enchanting depths, uncovering hidden truths and expanding our understanding of the intricate interplay between numbers and the universe.

May this compilation serve as a catalyst, stirring the flames of curiosity within every soul who dares to inquire. For it is through our collective pursuit of knowledge that we unlock the boundless wonders of numerology, nurturing a deeper connection to the profound mysteries that surround us all.

PRIYANKA KUUMAR

TABLE OF CONTENTS

CHAPTER 1

THE FOUNDATIONS OF NUMEROLOGY: EXPLORING THE BASICS

In this chapter, we will embark on a captivating journey to unravel the essence of numerology and its profound impact on our existence. We will delve into the very core of numerology, exploring its workings and discovering how numbers can define us in ways we never imagined.

Does numerology predict your future? Is it possible that the numbers in our lives guide us towards a predestined path? We'll explore these fascinating questions and ponder whether we are simply programmed beings, or if we have the power to shape our destinies.

But how accurate is numerology, and should you rely on it for crucial decisions? The reliability of numerology has been a subject of intrigue, and we'll explore the factors that influence its accuracy and how it can be a valuable tool for better self-awareness.

Are you wondering about the right age to explore numerology's secrets? We'll discover when is the optimal time to unlock the hidden meanings of numbers and how it can profoundly impact our lives.

As we delve into the world of numerology, we'll also explore its relationship with astrology, if any, and uncover its potential to analyse not only personal birth data but also the vibrations of names, places, and events.

Is numerology bound by religious beliefs, or does it transcend spiritual boundaries? We'll find out if numerology is universally applicable, irrespective of our faith or creed.

Which version of numerology should you use to explore your unique journey? We'll navigate through the various branches of numerology and help you find the one that resonates with you.

Finally, we'll also unveil how the study of numerology unravels the deeper patterns and meanings behind our life experiences, guiding us towards unparalleled self-awareness and personal growth.

Question 1: What is Numerology?

Numerology, a timeless practice rooted in ancient civilizations like Babylonia, Greece, Egypt, and India, holds the key to unravelling the profound significance of numbers and their influential power. Unlike complex mathematical equations, numerology speaks a language accessible to all, offering invaluable insights into our lives.

Imagine numerology as a wise guide, a trusted navigator who helps us make informed decisions and gain a deeper understanding of our own unique personality and life journey. By delving into the mystical world of numbers, we can tap into a wealth of knowledge that extends beyond the mundane.

Whether we seek guidance in matters of career, finance, relationships, or personal growth, numerology can illuminate our path. It unveils the hidden connections between our names, birth dates, and the numbers associated with them. In doing so, numerology sheds light on our inherent strengths and weaknesses, allowing us to embrace our true potential.

In the hustle and bustle of life, numerology serves as a profound tool to unravel the mysteries that lie within us. It enables us to make more conscious choices, leading to a more fulfilling and purposeful existence. By embracing numerology's wisdom, we empower ourselves to navigate life's twists and turns with clarity and confidence.

Question 2: How does Numerology work?

Numerology operates much like a GPS, providing guidance by exploring the potential and obstacles associated with individual numbers. In simple terms, numerology works by:

1. **Enhancing Positivity and Good Luck:** By making your name more auspicious and favourable, numerology brings forth positivity and good fortune. It is not uncommon to notice famous personalities making minor name changes based on numerological principles to attract positive vibrations and unlock favourable opportunities.

2. **Guiding Career Success and Satisfaction:** Numerology acts as a guiding force in determining the right line of work. By understanding the numerical energies related to different professions, numerology steers individuals towards fulfilling and harmonious career choices, resulting in success, satisfaction, and peace of mind.

3. **Creating Positive Energy in Surroundings:** Numerology extends its influence beyond personal aspects by also impacting our immediate environment. It assesses factors such as house numbers, office addresses, or company logos to create positive and vibrant energy in our surroundings. This fosters happiness, joy, and contentment in our daily lives.

4. **Strengthening Relationships and Self-awareness:** Numerology helps in developing good relationships not only with others but also with ourselves. By uncovering our strengths and weaknesses through numerological analysis, we gain valuable insights into our own character. This new-found self-awareness empowers us to nurture positive qualities and work on areas that require growth, fostering better relationships overall.

5. **Guiding the Achievement of Dreams:** Numerology serves as a compass for realising our aspirations. It guides us to recognize and seize the right opportunities at the opportune moment. By aligning ourselves with the numerical vibrations that resonate with our dreams, numerology acts as a transformative tool in achieving our goals.

Question 3: How can Numbers define you?

Numerology holds the key to understanding how numbers can define us. It's remarkable how numbers seem to be a constant presence in our lives. Whether it's our PAN card number, Aadhar card number, roll number, the ward number we were born in, mobile number, employee number, passport number, house number, vehicle number, or even our account number- numbers surround us at every turn.

Have you ever wondered why certain numbers always seem to attract you or why you feel drawn towards them? Perhaps it's the seat number at a multiplex, an airline, or even a taxi number. You might have noticed a particular fondness for numbers like 4 or 8. Later, we'll delve deeper into the significance of these numbers.

Given the constant presence of numbers in our lives, it's only natural that they have an impact on us as well. The vibrations emitted by numbers carry a certain energy, be it positive or negative, which can influence us in various ways. Numerology helps us unravel the secrets behind these vibrations, allowing us to harness their power for our benefit.

By understanding the numerical significance associated with our personal details and experiences, numerology provides insights into our strengths, weaknesses, potentials, and challenges. It allows us to gain a deeper understanding of ourselves and the energetic forces that shape our lives.

Question 4: Does Numerology predict your future?

Numerology does not provide a direct prediction of your future. Rather, it empowers you to actively shape and create your own future. It serves as a valuable tool that offers insights into your inherent qualities, strengths, and weaknesses. By understanding these aspects of yourself, you gain a deeper understanding of the paths and opportunities that are most aligned with your true potential. Numerology guides you in making informed decisions, taking proactive steps, and harnessing the power of the numbers associated with your life. Ultimately, it is your actions and choices that shape your future, and numerology serves only as a guiding compass along the way.

Question 5: If numerology says so much about us, are we programmed?

Numerology reveals that we are indeed influenced by various factors such as planetary alignments, numbers, culture, social systems, and our upbringing. These influences play a significant role in shaping our thoughts, behaviour, opinions, attitudes, and emotions. However, it is crucial to understand that this programming does not define who we are but rather provides insights into what we can discover about ourselves and the purpose of our lives.

As human beings, we are complex and unique individuals, and no external force can dictate or restrict our lives without our consent. Numerology serves as a tool to help us become the best versions of ourselves. It allows us to gain a deeper understanding of our strengths, weaknesses, potentials, and challenges. By embracing this knowledge, we can make conscious choices, set our own path, and shape our own destiny.

Numerology empowers us to break free from limiting beliefs and societal expectations. It encourages us to explore our true potential, pursue our passions, and live a fulfilling life aligned with our individuality. Ultimately, it is our own choices, actions, and determination that shape our journey. Numerology acts as a guiding compass, helping us navigate the complexities of life and unleash our innate greatness.

Question 6: How accurate is numerology, and should I rely on it for important decisions?

Numerology is a valuable tool that offers insights and guidance, but its accuracy depends on how it is used and interpreted. While numerology can provide valuable insights, it is crucial to consider other factors when making important decisions. Hard work, intuition, logic, and common sense should all be taken into account alongside numerological guidance.

Numerology encourages positive changes in lifestyle and behaviour, but it is ultimately up to you to take action and make those changes. Just as medicine requires faith and belief to be effective, trusting yourself and having belief in your decisions is essential. Numerology can provide guidance, but you have the power to shape your own destiny.

When it comes to important decisions, it is wise to take a holistic approach. Consider numerology alongside other aspects of your life, such as your personal values, goals, and practical considerations. By combining various factors and trusting your own judgement, you can make informed decisions that align with your true desires and aspirations.

Question 7: What is the ideal age to get a numerology reading done?

It is recommended to get a numerology reading done as early as possible to benefit from the positive vibrations of an auspicious name. Some individuals even choose to have numerology reports prepared for newborn babies, allowing them to harness the numerological benefits from the very beginning of their lives. By getting a numerology reading at a young age, you can gain insights into your unique numerical influences and use that knowledge to navigate your life journey with a greater clarity and purpose. Whether you're starting a new chapter in life or seeking guidance for personal growth, the earlier you embrace numerology, the sooner you can unlock its potential to enhance your life's path.

Question 8: How does numerology relate to astrology, if at all?

Numerology and astrology are two ancient systems that offer insights into different aspects of life. Although they are distinct practices, there are connections and overlaps between the two.

Numerology focuses on the symbolism and vibrational energy of numbers. It assigns numerical values to letters and uses calculations based on these values to gain meaningful insights. Numerology highlights the significance of individual numbers and their impact on a person's personality, strengths, weaknesses, and other aspects of life.

Astrology, on the other hand, studies celestial bodies, such as planets, their positions and movements in relation with human affairs and personality traits. It divides the zodiac into twelve signs and examines the planetary placements at the time of birth to understand one's character, potential, and life events.

The connection between numerology and astrology lies in their shared recognition of the influence of numbers and planets on human life. Astrology often incorporates numerology as a complementary tool. For instance, the numerological significance of a person's birth date or name might be considered alongside their astrological chart for a more comprehensive understanding.

Furthermore, specific numbers in numerology are associated with particular celestial bodies. For example, the number 1 is often linked to the Sun, 2 to the Moon, and so on. These associations add extra layers of interpretation and meaning when analysing numerological charts or exploring the significance of certain numbers.

It's essential to understand that while numerology and astrology have similarities, they are separate disciplines with their unique approaches and techniques. Each system provides valuable insights and can be used individually or together to gain a deeper understanding of oneself and the world.

Question 9: Can numerology be applied to analyse the numerological vibrations of names, places, or events, in addition to personal birth data?

In numerology, the scope of application extends beyond personal birth data. Numerological analysis can be applied to names, places, and events to gain insights into their energetic vibrations and symbolic meanings. Here's how numerology can be used in these contexts:

1. **Name Analysis:** Numerology allows for analysis of the vibrations and influences of names. Each letter in a name corresponds to a numerical value, and by calculating these numbers and examining their interactions, a numerologist can glean insights into the personality traits, characteristics, strengths, and challenges associated with a person's name. This can be valuable in understanding how a name shapes one's identity and influences their life's path.

2. **Business or Brand Names:** Numerology can be employed to analyse the numerological vibrations of business or brand names. By assessing the numerical values of the letters and

determining the overall numerical energy of the name, numerologists can provide insights into the potential success, branding, and alignment of the name with the business's purpose or target audience. This analysis aids in selecting names that resonate positively with the intended goals and objectives.

3. **Location Analysis:** Numerology can also be utilised to analyse the numerological vibrations of specific places or addresses. By calculating the numerical values associated with the letters or numbers in an address or location name, numerologists can gain insights into the energetic qualities and influences of that place. This is particularly relevant when choosing a new home, office, or vacation destination, as it provides a deeper understanding of the energy and compatibility of the location with an individual or the purpose.

4. **Event Timing:** Numerology can be employed to analyse the numerological vibrations of specific dates or events. By calculating the numerical values associated with the date or event, numerologists can offer insights into the potential energies, themes, and opportunities that may be present during that time. This analysis can be beneficial for selecting auspicious dates for weddings, initiating new projects, or making important decisions.

By applying numerology to names, places, and events, individuals and businesses can gain a deeper understanding of the symbolic meanings, energetic influences, and potential outcomes associated with them. This knowledge empowers them to make informed decisions, foster alignment, and create positive and harmonious environments or experiences.

Question 10: Is numerology related to any particular religion?

Numerology is not tied to any particular religion and can be practised independent of religious affiliations. People from different religious backgrounds can explore numerology as a means of self-reflection, personal development, and gaining valuable insights into different facets of life.

It is a versatile tool that can be embraced by individuals seeking a deeper understanding of themselves and the world around them, regardless of their religious beliefs. Numerology transcends religious boundaries and offers a unique perspective that can be applied universally.

Question 11: Which numerology system do you follow?

I mainly follow the Chaldean method of numerology, which is considered to be one of the oldest and most respected system of numbers, with its origins dating back to ancient Babylon around 4004 BCE. However, when examining an individual's name and numbers for their numerology analysis, I incorporate the Pythagorean and Chinese systems in my assessment process as well, as I personally believe that one should embrace the best of everything and follow a holistic approach.

Question 12: Is numerology solely based on the date of birth?

Numerology primarily uses your date of birth and original name to create a personal numerology report. However, if someone doesn't know their original date of birth, numerology can still be applied by analysing and correcting their name, signature, mobile number, and other aspects according to general auspicious numbers. These additional elements can provide insights and align the individual's numerological vibrations with favourable energies for a harmonious and balanced life.

Numerology offers flexibility in its application, allowing various factors to be considered and adjusted to enhance the accuracy and effectiveness of the analysis.

Question 13: How does the study of numerology help us in understanding the deeper patterns and meanings behind our life experiences and how does it guide us towards greater self-awareness and personal growth?

The study of numerology offers us a deeper understanding of the patterns and meanings in our life experiences, leading to greater self-awareness and personal growth. It does this in several significant ways:

1. **Discovering Life Themes:** Numerology examines our birthdate and name to reveal the underlying energies that shape our lives. By understanding our strengths, challenges, and life purpose, we can make sense of recurring patterns and life lessons.

2. **Gaining Self-Reflection and Insight:** Numerology encourages self-reflection by prompting us to explore the significance of numbers in our lives. This process fosters self-awareness, allowing us to identify areas for personal growth.

3. **Improving Decision-Making:** Numerology provides a framework for making informed decisions that align with our unique vibrational qualities. It helps us make choices that resonate with our authentic selves and life purpose.

4. **Understanding Relationships:** Numerology offers insights into the dynamics of our relationships. By comparing numerological profiles, we gain a deeper understanding of compatibility and challenges, leading to improved communication and harmony.

5. **Empowering Personal Growth:** Numerology is a powerful tool for personal development. Recognizing our strengths and challenges enables us to focus on self-improvement and reach our potential.

6. **Aligning with Life Purpose:** Numerology helps uncover our life purpose and guides us towards fulfilling it. By understanding our life path's numeric vibrations, we can make

conscious choices that support our spiritual and personal growth.

CHAPTER 2

DEMYSTIFYING NUMEROLOGY: ANSWERING COMMON QUESTIONS AND MISCONCEPTIONS

In this chapter, we aim to uncover the truth behind some of the most intriguing questions and misconceptions surrounding the enigmatic world of numerology!

Have you ever wondered how birthplace plays a role in shaping your numerological profile? Can a simple spelling mistake on your birth certificate have significant implications from a numerological perspective? We'll explore these aspects and reveal the hidden influences that birth details can have on our numerological journey.

Some numbers are believed to bestow an easier life upon individuals. But which numbers are they, and what makes them special? And what about the elusive concept of a "lucky number"? Is there really a number that can bring good fortune?

Superstitions often surround the number 13, labelling it as unlucky. Is it just a cultural belief, or does the number hold a deeper significance in numerology? We'll uncover the truth behind this age-old superstition.

The absence of number 6 in an individual's numerological chart may hold intriguing implications. How might this missing number influence their personality traits, relationships, and approach to various aspects of life?

Why are certain dates, such as the 8th, 17th, and 26th considered inauspicious for auspicious work? We'll explore the beliefs and reasons behind these practices.

Birth dates for caesarean births can be chosen. But what factors should parents consider when making this critical decision, and how might this affect the child's life?

Encounters with Shani or Saturn can be daunting. But should we approach them with fear, or is there a more empowering mindset we should cultivate?

Even the selection of a simple Display Picture (DP) on your mobile device could hold numerological significance, shaping your personal energy and resonating with your unique vibrations.

In a world of readily available online resources, is it wise to rely solely on them for correcting your name numerologically? Or should you seek the guidance of a professional numerologist for more accurate and personalised insights?

Get ready to quench your curiosity as we unravel the mysteries, misconceptions associated with numerology.

Question 14: How does birthplace impact a person's numerological profile and what role does it play in numerology?

Birthplace holds a significant role in numerology as it influences a person's overall numerological profile. According to numerological beliefs, the birthplace carries its unique energy and vibrations that shape an individual's life journey and personality traits.

Different geographical locations and cultural contexts have their own distinct energies, which can impact a person's experiences and opportunities. The birthplace's energy interacts with an individual's numerological numbers, such as the birthdate and name, to shape their destiny.

For example, individuals born under zodiac signs associated with the element of Earth, like Taurus, Virgo, and Capricorn, may find a sense of belonging and stability by living in or near their birthplace. This is because the element of Earth is believed to be grounded, practical, and connected to the physical world. Being in proximity to the birthplace's energy can enhance these qualities and create a harmonious environment for personal growth.

Additionally, birthplace's energy can influence a person's compatibility with certain locations or cultures. Numerology suggests that certain birthplaces may resonate more strongly with an individual's numerological profile, aligning them with favourable circumstances and opportunities.

Question 15: What should I do from a numerological perspective if there is a spelling mistake on my birth certificate?

If you discover a spelling mistake on your birth certificate and are concerned about its impact from a numerological perspective, there are a few actions and considerations you can take:

1. **Numerological Analysis:** Seek the guidance of a numerologist who can analyse the effects of the spelling mistake on your numerological profile. They can assess whether the incorrect spelling has any significant impact on the numbers associated with your birth date or name.

2. **Name Numerology:** In numerology, the vibrations and energies associated with names are important. If the spelling mistake alters the pronunciation or numerical value of your name, it could potentially affect your numerological profile. A numerologist can evaluate the changes and provide advice on

whether adjustments to the spelling of your name might be beneficial.

3. **Numerological Compatibility:** Numerology also takes into account the compatibility between different aspects of your birth date and name. If the spelling mistake disrupts the harmonious balance or compatibility within your numerological profile, it may be worth considering corrective measures.

Question 16: Are there certain numbers in numerology that can make life easier for individuals?

Numerology acknowledges that each number carries both positive and negative aspects. The purpose of understanding the positive and negative aspects of numbers is to cultivate awareness and balance, embracing the positive qualities while being mindful of the potential pitfalls or challenges associated with each number.

While no number guarantees a completely effortless life, certain numbers are often associated with qualities that can contribute to a more comfortable and smoother life. However, the ease of life is not solely determined by the number itself. It depends on the association of numbers with your own individual number, name, and your Karma.

Ultimately, living a fulfilling life involves a combination of personal effort, attitude, and alignment with one's values, rather than relying solely on the influence of a particular number in numerology.

Question 17: Are there any specific numbers in numerology that are commonly considered "lucky numbers"?

In numerology, the notion of a "lucky number" is subjective and varies from person to person. Although there is no universally agreed-upon lucky number, some numbers have been traditionally associated with good fortune and positive energies. However, the determination of lucky and unlucky numbers depends on an individual's date of birth and their numerological profile.

Question 18: Is number 13 really an unlucky number, or is it just a superstition?

1. **Historical Origins:** The belief in number 13 being unlucky has historical roots. For example, in Christian tradition, 13 is associated with the Last Supper, where Judas, the betrayer of Jesus, was the 13th guest. This association with betrayal and the subsequent crucifixion of Jesus has contributed to the negative perception of the number 13.

2. **Cultural Superstitions:** Various cultures have their own superstitions regarding the number 13. For instance, in some Western societies, the fear of number 13 is called triskaidekaphobia. This fear has led to the avoidance of this number in building designs, hotel floors, or seating arrangements.

3. **Pop Culture Influence:** The perception of number 13 as unlucky has been perpetuated in popular culture, including books, movies, and folklore. This ongoing exposure to the idea of number 13 being associated with bad luck has reinforced the belief for many individuals.

4. **Confirmation Bias:** Once a belief is established, people tend to notice and remember events that confirm their preconceived notions. This phenomenon, known as confirmation bias, can lead individuals to attribute negative occurrences to number 13, reinforcing the belief in its unlucky nature. For example, the Jallianwala Bagh massacre took place on 13th April 1919, the parliament was attacked on 13th December 2001, serial blasts ensued on Mumbai trains on 13th March 2003 and fires started at Uphaar Cinema in Delhi on Friday, the 13th of June 1997, amongst other incidents.

5. **Individual Experiences:** Personal experiences and anecdotes can also shape one's perception of the number 13. If someone has encountered challenging or unfortunate situations on a Friday the 13th, for example, they may associate those events with the number and as a consequence, consider it unlucky.

6. **Cultural Variation:** It's worth noting that beliefs about number 13 vary across cultures. In some cultures, such as Chinese or Indian, number 13 is not inherently considered unlucky. Cultural variations highlight that the perception of luck and misfortune is subjective and influenced by cultural and societal norms.

Question 19: What happens when number 6 is missing from someone's numerological chart? How does this absence affect their personality, relationships, and approach to life?

When the number 6 is missing from an individual's numerological chart, several implications arise. Firstly, they may face difficulty connecting with their own emotions, making it challenging for them to understand and address the emotional needs of others in their relationships.

Secondly, achieving a harmonious balance between their professional responsibilities and personal life could be a struggle. This imbalance may lead to added stress and difficulty in managing work-life commitments.

Moreover, the absence of number 6 may indicate a reduced inclination towards community engagement and a decreased desire to actively participate in social gatherings or events like parties and weddings.

Overall, the lack of number 6 in the numerological chart may impact the concerned person's emotional well-being, relationships, and social interactions.

Question 20: What number is typically missing from an individual's numerological profile if they lack willpower, courage, and passion?

If someone lacks willpower, courage, and passion, it often indicates the absence of number 9 in their numerological profile. Number 9 is associated with traits like determination, strength, and a strong sense of purpose. Its absence may suggest a lack of drive, difficulty in facing challenges, and a reduced enthusiasm for life.

Individuals without number 9 may struggle to find motivation and assertiveness needed to overcome obstacles and achieve success. They might also find it challenging to connect with their true passions and feel disconnected from their deeper desires. To enhance these qualities, it's essential for them to work on building their willpower, finding a sense of purpose, and embracing courage in their endeavours. Developing self-belief and a positive outlook can also help them unleash their inner potential and lead a fulfilling life.

Question 21: What are the reasons or beliefs behind the practice of avoiding auspicious work on the dates 8, 17, and 26?

In Numerology, number 8 is associated with planet Saturn. Saturn is often known as the planet of judgement. It seeks strict discipline and responsibility from individuals or else it limits success and rewards. It is believed that on dates that add up to 8 (like 8th, 17th, or 26th of any month), the influence of Saturn may bring challenges, delays, or obstacles to certain activities.

Over time, there have been many tragic incidents that have occurred on these dates, reinforcing the apprehension surrounding these numbers. For example, the terrorist attacks in Mumbai happened on 26th November 2008 and the Mumbai floods on 26th July 2005. Similarly, an earthquake struck Gujarat on 26th January 2001 and the 2008 Ahmedabad bombings happened on 26th July. Also, the devastating Indian Ocean Tsunami in 2004 transpired on the 26th of December that year. The Kashmir earthquake in 2005 happened on 8th October. Furthermore, Malaysian Airlines Flight 17 was shot down and subsequently crashed on 17th July 2014. The same year, another Malaysian Airlines flight had disappeared on 8th March.

However, it's essential to understand that the impact of Saturn's influence can vary for each person, depending on their individual birth chart and other astrological / numerological factors. While the energy of Saturn might indicate the need for patience and a structured approach, it can also offer opportunities for growth, endurance, and developing a strong sense of responsibility.

Question 22: Is it possible for parents to have a choice in selecting a specific date for a caesarean birth, and what factors might be considered in making such a decision?

Parents may express their preferences for a specific date for caesarean birth based on numerology. However, it's crucial to understand that medical considerations take precedence in such decisions. The timing of a caesarean birth is primarily determined by the mother's health condition and the baby's well-being. Medical professionals will assess factors such as the baby's lung maturity and gestational age to ensure a safe delivery.

While personal beliefs are valued, the final decision rests on the advice and expertise of healthcare providers, prioritising the health and safety of both, the mother and the baby.

Question 23: Do we need to approach the influence of Shani or Saturn with fear, and what mindset should be cultivated when encountering their effects?

Approaching the influence of Shani or Saturn with fear is not necessary. Though Saturn's energy can bring challenges and limitations, it's crucial to maintain a mindset of respect, understanding, and resilience when encountering its effects.

Instead of being fearful, adopting a mindset of acceptance and learning can be much more beneficial. Embracing the lessons and growth opportunities that Saturn presents while maintaining a proactive and disciplined approach, will help you navigate its influence with a positive outlook. Remember, Saturn's influence can lead to personal development, wisdom, and long-term rewards. By keeping a balanced perspective and working diligently, you can tackle the influence of Shani or Saturn with a positive mindset.

1. **Acceptance of challenges:** Rather than fearing or resisting the obstacles brought by Saturn, embrace them as opportunities for growth and learning. Saturn's lessons often lead to greater maturity, wisdom, and inner strength.

2. **Patience and perseverance:** Saturn teaches the virtues of patience and endurance. Understand that positive results may take time to manifest. Be patient and persistent in your efforts, knowing that Saturn rewards diligent, honest, and consistent work overtime.

3. **Personal responsibility:** Take ownership of your actions, decisions, and their consequences. Embrace a proactive mindset and make responsible choices that align with your long-term goals.

4. **Self-discipline and structure:** Cultivate self-discipline in your daily life by establishing routines, setting goals, and prioritising tasks. Create a sense of order and organisation to make the most of Saturn's energy.

5. **Seek balance and self-care:** While Saturn encourages hard work and responsibility, it's equally important to maintain balance in all aspects of life. Prioritise self-care activities, relaxation, and leisure to prevent burnout and maintain a healthy balance.

6. **Learn from Saturn's lessons:** Reflect on past experiences and challenges brought by Saturn. Identify the lessons learned and use this knowledge to navigate future challenges with a greater understanding.

7. **Respect and honour elderly individuals:** Show respect and honour towards elderly individuals, especially your parents and grandparents. Seek their guidance and wisdom, and demonstrate gratitude for their presence in your life. By valuing and respecting the elderly, you align yourself with Saturn's energy.

8. **Engage in acts of service and charity:** Saturn appreciates acts of selflessness and service to others. Volunteer your time, skills, or resources to charitable causes or organisations. Help those in need or engage in random acts of kindness. By demonstrating compassion and serving others, you please Saturn's energy.

Question 24: Does selecting a particular Display Picture (DP) on your mobile device hold any numerological significance in shaping your personal energy and resonating with your unique vibrations?

The selection of a Display Picture (DP) on your mobile device may not have direct numerological significance, but it can still play a role in shaping your personal energy and resonating with your unique vibrations. While numerology focuses on numbers and their influences, the images we choose to display on our mobile devices can have subconscious effects on our emotions and mindset.

When selecting a DP, consider choosing images that promote positive emotions and a sense of well-being. Opt for pictures that evoke happiness, serenity, or positivity. Surrounding yourself with uplifting visuals can contribute to an increased positive mindset throughout the day. These images can act as reminders of your goals, aspirations, values, or moments of happiness, providing motivation and inspiration when you interact with your mobile device.

A DP can also reflect your personality and interests, allowing you to express yourself and showcase your uniqueness. By choosing images that resonate with your true self, you create a visual representation of your identity and values. This alignment between your DP and your authentic self can contribute to a sense of harmony and positivity in your daily life.

Question 25: Is it advisable to solely rely on online sources for correcting my name numerologically, or is it necessary to consult with a professional numerologist for accurate and personalised guidance?

When it comes to correcting your name numerologically, it's essential to approach online sources with caution. While the internet provides a wealth of information on numerology and name corrections, the subject itself is complex and requires a deep understanding of numerical vibrations and their influences.

For accurate and personalised guidance, it is advisable to consult with a professional numerologist. These experts have in-depth knowledge of numerology and can provide specific recommendations based on your individual name and birth details. By analysing the numbers associated with your name and birth date, they can offer valuable insights and suggest potential modifications if needed.

A professional numerologist takes into account various factors to provide informed advice. They consider your birth date, current name, and desired outcomes to tailor their recommendations to your unique situation. This personalised approach ensures that the changes you make to your name align harmoniously with your life's path and aspirations.

While online resources can offer general information and insights into numerology, they may not be able to provide the level of depth and accuracy that a one-on-one consultation with a qualified numerologist can offer. Making significant changes to your name without proper guidance can lead to unintended consequences, so it's crucial to seek expert advice.

CHAPTER 3

DECODING THE DIGITS: MASTERING NUMEROLOGICAL CALCULATIONS

Welcome to a chapter that holds the key to unlocking the secrets hidden within numbers – Decoding the Digits! Have you ever wondered how numbers can reveal fascinating insights about our lives? In this chapter, we'll unravel the mysteries behind some fundamental numerological calculations that hold the power to define our destiny.

Discover the magic behind calculating your destiny number, a unique code that holds the essence of your life's purpose and potential. But that's not all – we'll also explore the significance of your birth number, a special number that shapes your personality and influences your life's journey.

Numbers surround us every day, and did you know that each day of the week also has a corresponding number? We'll delve into this intriguing aspect and see how the days of the week are interconnected with numerology.

Moreover, we'll introduce you to the concept of the Personal Year in Numerology. Discover how this dynamic number can provide valuable insights into the themes and energies that will influence you every year in a different way.

Question 26: How is the Destiny Number calculated in Numerology?

In numerology, the destiny number is calculated by adding the digits of an individual's full and original date of birth and reducing the sum to a single digit.

To calculate your destiny number, follow these simple steps:

1. Write down your full date of birth in the format: dd/mm/yyyy (for example, if your birthday is on January 16th, 2000; you would write it as 16/01/2000).

2. Add together all of the digits in your birth date i.e., $1+6+0+1+2+0+0+0 = 10$

3. Reduce the sum to a single digit by adding the digits together again. In this example, you would add $1+0 = 1$.

4. If the final number is still a two-digit number, repeat step 3 until you get a single-digit number.

Question 27: How is Birth Number calculated in Numerology?

In numerology, birth number or personality number is the date you were born on (reduced to a single digit), excluding the month and the year.

Calculating your birth number in numerology is a simple process. Here's how you can do it:

1. Write down your complete date of birth in the format dd/mm/yyyy.

2. For example, let's say your date of birth is March 24th, 1981.

3. In this case, you would add the digits of the day you were born. In this example, 2 + 4 equals 6.

4. Your birth number is 6.

Question 28: How are numbers associated with each day of the week?

In numerology, each day of the week is linked to a specific number, adding an extra layer of significance to our daily lives.

Here is the numerical association for each day of the week:

- Sunday: 1-4

- Monday: 2-7

- Tuesday: 9

- Wednesday: 5

- Thursday: 3

- Friday: 6

- Saturday: 8

These numbers provide insight into the energetic qualities and vibrations of each day. They can influence our experiences, interactions, and decision-making. By understanding the numerical associations of the days, we can tap into their unique characteristics and align our activities accordingly. This knowledge allows us to make the most of each day, leveraging its specific energy and maximising our potential for success and fulfilment.

Question 29: Do alphabets have corresponding numbers in Numerology?

Yes, in Numerology, alphabets are assigned numerical values. These numerical values provide insights into the energetic qualities and vibrations associated with different letters.

In the Chaldean system, numbers 1 to 8 are given individual numerical values based on the vibration of the letters in the English alphabet. Number 9 is not used in the Chaldean system because it was considered to be a sacred number and was believed to have its own unique properties that did not align with other numbers.

As per this system, alphabetical letters are assigned the following numerical values:

$1 = A, I, J, Q, Y$

$2 = B, K, R$

$3 = C, G, L, S$

$4 = D, M, T$

$5 = E, H, N, X$

$6 = U, V, W$

$7 = O, Z$

$8 = F, P$

By understanding the numerical values of the letters in a person's name or words, Numerologists can analyse and interpret the underlying energies and influences. This information can offer valuable insights into a person's personality, strengths, challenges, and overall compatibility with others.

Question 30: How many numbers are considered in Numerology?

In Numerology, we focus on a total of nine numbers that form the foundation of all calculations and interpretations. These numbers are 1, 2, 3, 4, 5, 6, 7, 8, and 9. These single-digit numbers hold unique vibrations and symbolism, representing various aspects of life, personality traits, and energetic influences.

While there are numbers beyond nine, Numerology simplifies them by reducing them to their single-digit form. For example, 10 is reduced to 1 (1 + 0 = 1), and 11 is reduced to 2 (1 + 1 = 2). This reduction allows us to maintain the focus on the core energies and meanings associated with the nine fundamental numbers.

By understanding and working with these nine numbers, Numerology practitioners gain profound insights into different aspects of life, including personality, relationships, career, and spiritual growth. The simplicity and depth of these numbers make Numerology a powerful tool for self-discovery, guidance, and personal transformation.

Question 31: What makes the birth number so significant in numerology?

The birth number holds great importance in numerology due to several reasons. Firstly, it is a number that remains unchanged throughout a person's life, representing a constant influence. Secondly, birth number is associated with the planetary energies present on the day of birth, which can shape an individual's characteristics and experiences. It holds a connection to the material aspects of life, such as career, finances, and practical endeavours.

Numerologists believe that the birth number provides valuable insights into a person's core personality traits, strengths, and tendencies. It serves as a foundation for understanding an individual's natural inclinations, behavioural patterns, and potential direction of life. By analysing the birth number, numerologists can gain a deeper understanding of a person's unique qualities and find insights about their life journey and potential challenges they may encounter.

Overall, birth number acts as a fundamental building block in numerology, forming the basis for further calculations and interpretations. It offers a glimpse into the essential aspects of an individual's character and helps uncover their inherent traits, contributing to a comprehensive understanding of their numerological profile.

Question 32: What is a Personal Year in Numerology? How is it calculated?

In numerology, the idea or concept of a personal year is based on the belief that each year of your life is associated with a particular energy or vibration that influences your experiences and opportunities.

To calculate your personal year, you add your birth month and birth date to the current year.

For example – if your date of birth is 24th June, 1977, this can be written as 24/ 6/1977.

To calculate Personal Year in 2023 – you add $24 + 6 + 2023 = 19$.

Now reduce the total to a single digit which comes to - $1+9 = 10$ and then $1+0 = 1$.

In this way, the year 2023 is personal year 1 for the individual whose date of birth is 24th June 1977.

Each personal year holds a specific meaning in numerology as explained below:

1. **Personal Year 1:** As this year is governed by Sun, things related to father, father figure or fatherhood can occur. This

year represents new beginnings, fresh starts, upholding your independence, setting goals for the future, and opportunities for personal growth.

2. **Personal Year 2:** This year is governed by Moon. The focus of this year is on relationships, mother or motherhood related events, cooperation, emotions, imaginative temperament, romance, partnerships, and harmony. It's a year to develop patience and diplomacy.

3. **Personal Year 3:** This year is ruled by Jupiter, which is the planet of expansion. This year is characterised by creativity, self-expression, communication, expansion in all aspects, and social activities. This is the year to be more calm, collected, and creative.

4. **Personal Year 4:** This is the year of sudden changes, unexpected developments. The energy of this year is to be grounded, practical, and focused on building a solid foundation. It's the time for hard work, discipline, and paying attention to details.

5. **Personal Year 5:** This year brings a sense of adventure, freedom, and change. It's the time for exploration, embracing new experiences, and taking calculated risks. Flexibility, adaptability, and openness to change are crucial. Commercial undertakings, buying, selling, writing, increased travel, worrying, and restless temperament will be the highlight of this year.

6. **Personal Year 6:** The emphasis of this year is on home, family, and responsibility. It's the time to nurture relationships, create harmony in your domestic life, and focus on your caregiving abilities. Love, marriage, and parenthood may be highlighted.

7. **Personal Year 7:** This year encourages introspection, spiritual growth, and self-reflection. It's the time for solitude, research, and inner exploration. Developing your intuition, studying, and seeking deeper truths. Loss, any kind of separation, illness, misunderstandings may occur this year.

8. **Personal Year 8:** You may see slow results, delay, frustration. This year is associated with financial success, and personal power too. This is the year for career advancements, financial planning, focus, ambition, ethical conduct, being creative and constructive.

9. **Personal Year 9:** The energy of this year revolves around completion and closing of a nine-year cycle, which indicates the end of one style of living, and the beginning of a new chapter of life. It's a time for endings, forgiveness, and serving others. Reflect on the lessons learned and prepare for a new cycle ahead.

CHAPTER 4

UNVEILING YOUR ESSENCE: UNDERSTANDING PERSONALITY IN NUMEROLOGICAL TERMS

In this chapter, we are embarking on a journey to explore the fascinating traits and characteristics of people based on their date of birth. We are going to cover all dates of the month - from 1st to 31st!

We will also explore the correlations between birth numbers and destinies, uncover the positive and negative aspects of each number, and even examine how an individual's birth number might influence their musical preferences.

Question 33: In numerology, what are the traits and characteristics associated with individuals having birth number 1 i.e., people who are born on the 1st, 10th, 19th, and 28th?

Individuals born on the 1st, 10th, 19th, and 28th of a month are associated with birth number 1 in numerology and possess distinct traits and characteristics. Here are some key traits of people born on these dates:

1. **Independence:** People with birth number 1 value their independence and self-reliance. They prefer to take charge of their own lives and make decisions without relying heavily on others.

2. **Leadership:** Individuals with birth number 1 often exhibit natural leadership qualities. They have a strong sense of confidence, assertiveness, and the ability to guide and inspire others towards success.

3. **Ambition:** Those born with birth number 1 are highly ambitious individuals. They have a strong drive to achieve their goals and are motivated to excel in their chosen endeavours.

4. **Creativity:** People associated with birth number 1 tend to possess a creative and innovative mindset. They have original thinking abilities and can come up with unique ideas and solutions.

5. **Courage:** Birth number 1 individuals are known for their courage and willingness to take risks. They have the bravery to step out of their comfort zones and pursue their passions despite uncertainties.

6. **Self-confidence:** Individuals with birth number 1 typically have a high level of self-confidence. They believe in their abilities, have faith in their own judgement, and are not easily swayed by others' opinions.

7. **Individuality:** People with birth number 1 value their individuality and enjoy being different from the crowd. They embrace their unique perspectives and are not afraid to stand out.

8. **Determination:** Those with birth number 1 are characterised by their strong determination and persistence. They possess the

inner strength to overcome obstacles, and they continue moving forward despite challenges.

9. **Success-oriented:** Birth number 1 individuals are focused on achieving success in their chosen fields. They strive for excellence and are willing to put in the necessary effort and hard work to accomplish their objectives.

10. **Initiative:** People associated with birth number 1 are proactive and take initiative in various aspects of life. They are not afraid to start new projects or take the lead in challenging situations.

Question 34: In numerology, what are the traits and characteristics associated with individuals having birth number 2 i.e., people who are born on the 2nd, 11th, 20th, and 29th?

People born on the 2nd, 11th, 20th and 29th of a month are represented by birth number 2 in numerology and possess unique traits and qualities. Let's explore some of the characteristics commonly associated with these individuals:

1. **Cooperation:** Birth number 2 individuals have a cooperative nature and excel in team environments. They value collaboration and work well with others, bringing a diplomatic and harmonious approach to their interactions.

2. **Sensitivity:** People with birth number 2 are often highly sensitive and empathetic. They have a keen understanding of emotions and are attuned to the feelings of those around them. Their compassionate nature enables them to connect deeply with others.

3. **Balance:** Birth number 2 individuals seek balance and harmony in all aspects of their lives. They have a natural ability to find middle ground and resolve conflicts peacefully. Maintaining equilibrium is important to them.

4. **Partnership:** Individuals with birth number 2 thrive in partnerships and collaborations. They value meaningful relationships and excel in creating strong connections with others. They are skilled at fostering cooperation and teamwork.

5. **Support:** Birth number 2 individuals are known for their supportive and nurturing nature. They genuinely care about the well-being of others and enjoy helping, and encouraging them to achieve their goals. Their presence often brings comfort and reassurance.

Question 35: In numerology, what are the traits and characteristics associated with individuals having birth number 3 i.e., people who are born on the 3rd, 12th, 21st, and 30th?

Individuals born on the 3rd, 12th, 21st, and 30th of a month are represented by birth number 3 in numerology and possess distinct traits and qualities. Let's explore some of the characteristics commonly associated with these individuals:

1. **Creativity:** Birth number 3 people are known for their heightened creativity and artistic talents. They have a vivid imagination and often excel in artistic endeavours, such as writing, painting, and music.

2. **Communication:** Individuals with birth number 3 have excellent communication skills. They are expressive, charismatic, and have a natural flair for sharing their thoughts and ideas with others. They can captivate an audience with their words.

3. **Optimism:** People with birth number 3 are generally optimistic and have a positive outlook on life. They radiate positivity and have a cheerful disposition that can uplift the spirits of those around them. Their optimism helps them navigate challenges with resilience.

4. **Social:** Birth number 3 individuals are social butterflies. They thrive in social settings, enjoy meeting new people, and have a knack for making friends easily. They have a natural charm that attracts others to them.

5. **Joy:** People with birth number 3 often exude joy and bring a sense of fun to their surroundings. They have an infectious zest for life and find joy in the little things. Their vibrant energy and enthusiasm are contagious.

Question 36: In numerology, what are the traits and characteristics associated with individuals having birth number 4 i.e., people who are born on the 4th, 13th, 22nd, and 31st?

Individuals born on the 4th, 13th, 22nd, 31st of a month are represented by birth number 4 in numerology and possess unique traits and qualities. Let's explore some of the characteristics commonly associated with these individuals:

1. **Stability:** Birth number 4 individuals value stability and security in their lives. They are reliable, dependable, and work hard to create a solid foundation for themselves and their loved ones.

2. **Practicality:** People with birth number 4 have a practical and down-to-earth approach to life. They are grounded, logical, and excel in tasks that require attention to detail. Their practical mindset helps them find practical solutions to problems.

3. **Discipline:** Birth number 4 individuals have a strong sense of self-discipline. They are focused, determined, and committed to achieving their goals. They understand the importance of hard work and are willing to put in the necessary effort to succeed.

4. **Structure:** Individuals with birth number 4 thrive in structured environments. They appreciate routine, order, and organisation.

They have a natural ability to plan, strategize, and excel in careers that require structure and precision.

5. **Loyalty:** Birth number 4 people are known for their loyalty and reliability. They value trust and are committed to their commitments and relationships. They are steadfast. and make supportive friends and partners.

Question 37: In numerology, what are the traits and characteristics associated with individuals having birth number 5 i.e., people who are born on the 5th, 14th, and 23rd?

Individuals born on the 5th, 14th, and 23rd of a month are represented by birth number 5 in numerology and possess unique traits and qualities. Let's explore some of the characteristics commonly associated with these individuals:

1. **Adventure:** Birth number 5 individuals have a strong sense of adventure and a desire for freedom. They enjoy exploring new experiences, taking risks, and embracing change. They are open to new possibilities, and love to embark on exciting journeys.

2. **Adaptability:** People with birth number 5 are highly adaptable and flexible. They can easily adjust to different situations and thrive in dynamic environments. Their ability to adapt allows them to navigate through life's challenges with ease.

3. **Curiosity:** Birth number 5 individuals have a curious nature and a thirst for knowledge. They have a keen interest in learning and exploring diverse subjects. They enjoy intellectual stimulation and are constantly seeking new information and experiences.

4. **Variety:** Individuals with birth number 5 seek variety and excitement in life. They are attracted to diverse opportunities and enjoy engaging in multiple activities or pursuing different

interests simultaneously. They thrive in environments that offer them a range of options.

5. **Freedom:** Birth number 5 people value their freedom and independence. They resist being tied down and prefer to have the freedom to make their own choices. They have a strong need for personal autonomy, and enjoy the ability to explore life on their own terms.

Question 38: In numerology, what are the traits and characteristics associated with individuals having birth number 6 i.e., people who are born on the 6th, 15th, and 24th?

Individuals born on the 6th, 15th, and 24th of a month are represented by birth number 6 in numerology and possess unique traits and qualities. Let's explore some of the characteristics commonly associated with these individuals:

1. **Harmony**: Birth number 6 individuals have a strong sense of harmony and balance. They strive for peace and fairness in their relationships and surroundings. They have a natural ability to mediate conflicts and create a harmonious atmosphere.

2. **Responsibility:** People with birth number 6 are responsible and reliable. They take their commitments seriously and often take on caregiving roles. They are dependable, and can be counted on to fulfil their obligations.

3. **Compassion:** Birth number 6 individuals are compassionate and nurturing. They are often drawn to helping professions as they have deep empathy for others. They genuinely care about the well-being of those around them, and are willing to offer support and understanding.

4. **Family:** Individuals with birth number 6 place a strong emphasis on family and home. They value close-knit relationships and enjoy creating a nurturing environment. They

find fulfilment in taking care of their loved ones and creating a sense of belonging.

5. **Service:** Birth number 6 people have a natural inclination towards serving others. They find fulfilment in acts of kindness and making a positive difference in the lives of others. They often gravitate towards careers or activities that allow them to be of service to their community.

Question 39: In numerology, what are the traits and characteristics associated with individuals having birth number 7 i.e., people who are born on the 7th, 16th, and 25th?

Individuals born on the 7th, 16th, and 25th of a month are represented by birth number 7 in numerology and possess distinct traits and qualities. Let's explore some of the characteristics commonly associated with these individuals:

1. **Introspection:** Birth number 7 individuals are introspective and contemplative. They find solace in spending time alone and exploring their inner worlds. They have a deep sense of self-awareness, and enjoy delving into their thoughts and emotions.

2. **Wisdom:** People with birth number 7 have a profound well of wisdom and intuition. They trust their inner guidance and often have a spiritual or philosophical inclination. They possess a deep understanding of life, and are drawn to seeking knowledge and higher truths.

3. **Analysis:** Birth number 7 individuals are analytical and detail oriented. They have sharp minds and enjoy delving into complex subjects. They possess a natural ability to dissect information and draw insightful conclusions.

4. **Research:** Individuals with birth number 7 excel in research and investigation. They have a natural curiosity and enjoy

uncovering hidden truths. They have a keen eye for detail and are skilled at unravelling mysteries.

5. **Solitude:** Birth number 7 people appreciate solitude, and often require time alone to recharge and reflect. They find inner peace and clarity when they have moments of quiet introspection. Solitude is vital for their overall well-being.

Question 40: In numerology, what are the traits and characteristics associated with individuals having birth number 8 i.e., people who are born on the 8th, 17th, and 26th?

Individuals born on the 8th, 17th, and 26th of a month are represented by the birth number 8 in numerology and possess distinct traits and qualities. Let's explore some of the characteristics commonly associated with these individuals:

1. **Ambition:** Birth number 8 individuals are highly ambitious and driven. They have an intense desire for success and are willing to put in the effort required to achieve their goals. They possess a relentless determination to reach the pinnacle of success.

2. **Power:** People with birth number 8 often exude a natural magnetism and presence. They are drawn to positions of power and leadership, and their inherent charisma can inspire and influence others.

3. **Abundance:** Birth number 8 individuals have a strong connection with material abundance and financial success. They possess the potential for great prosperity, and are often driven to create wealth and enjoy the finer things in life.

4. **Authority:** Individuals with birth number 8 naturally carry an air of authority. They have a commanding presence and can take charge of situations with confidence. Others respect their opinions and value their leadership.

5. **Achievement:** Birth number 8 people are highly focused on achieving significant accomplishments. They set high

standards for themselves and are determined to excel in their endeavours. They have a strong work ethic, and are willing to overcome challenges to achieve their goals.

Question 41: In numerology, what are the traits and characteristics associated with individuals having birth number 9 i.e., people who are born on the 9th, 18th, and 27th?

Individuals born on the 9th, 18th, and 27th of a month are represented by the birth number 9 in numerology and exhibit unique traits and qualities. Let's delve into the characteristics commonly associated with these individuals:

1. **Compassion**: Birth number 9 individuals possess a deep well of compassion and empathy. They have a genuine concern for the well-being of others, and feel a strong desire to contribute to the betterment of humanity.

2. **Philanthropy**: People with birth number 9 often have a philanthropic nature. They feel a calling to help others and make a positive impact on society. They are driven by a sense of altruism and find fulfilment in acts of generosity.

3. **Idealism**: Birth number 9 individuals have a strong sense of idealism and vision for a better world. They are passionate advocates for social justice, equality, and the welfare of all beings. They strive to create positive change in their communities and beyond.

4. **Wisdom**: Individuals with birth number 9 possess a deep wisdom and understanding of life. They have gained valuable insights through their experiences and often offer profound advice and guidance to others. Their broad perspective allows them to see the bigger picture.

5. **Completion**: Birth number 9 people are associated with endings and the culmination of cycles. They have a transformative energy and often go through personal

transformations. They embrace change, and are adept at navigating transitions in life.

Question 42: Is it probable for two individuals who share the same date of birth to have similar destinies?

The probability of two individuals who share the same date of birth having similar destinies is not certain. While it may seem intriguing to think that sharing a birthdate could result in similar life paths, the reality is more complex.

Destinies are shaped by a multitude of factors, including personal choices, upbringing, education, environment, and life experiences. These factors create unique circumstances for each individual, influencing their decisions and opportunities along the way. Even small variations in these factors can lead to significant differences in life outcomes.

Additionally, every person possesses their own set of talents, strengths, specific name, signature, personal numbers (mobile, house, vehicle etc.) and aspirations that contribute to their individual journey. While sharing a birthdate may create a sense of connection or commonality, it does not necessarily dictate similar destinies.

Therefore, it is important to recognize that while two individuals may share the same date of birth, their paths in life can diverge significantly, making each person's journey distinct and personal.

Question 43: What are some positive and negative aspects of numbers in numerology?

Numerology attributes both positive and negative aspects to each number, shaping our understanding of their influence on our lives.

1. **Number 1:** Positive aspects include independence, leadership, and determination. Negative aspects encompass self-

centeredness, egotism, and a tendency to be overly ambitious or controlling.

2. **Number 2:** Positive aspects include cooperation, diplomacy, and sensitivity. Negative aspects involve indecisiveness, dependency, and a fear of confrontation.

3. **Number 3**: Positive aspects include creativity, self-expression, and sociability. Negative aspects entail scattered energy, superficiality, and a tendency to be overly dramatic or self-indulgent.

4. **Number 4:** Positive aspects include practicality, stability, and hard work. Negative aspects encompass rigidity, stubbornness, and a resistance to change or new ideas.

5. **Number 5:** Positive aspects include adaptability, freedom, and adventure. Negative aspects involve restlessness, impulsiveness, and a tendency to be scattered or irresponsible.

6. **Number 6:** Positive aspects include nurturing, compassion, and a strong sense of responsibility. Negative aspects encompass an overprotective nature, self-sacrifice to the point of neglecting oneself, and a tendency to meddle in others' affairs.

7. **Number 7:** Positive aspects include introspection, intuition, and spiritual awareness. Negative aspects involve isolation, aloofness, and a tendency to be overly analytical or sceptical.

8. **Number 8:** Positive aspects include ambition, financial success, and practicality. Negative aspects encompass materialism, workaholism, and a focus on power or control at the expense of personal relationships.

9. **Number 9:** Positive aspects include compassion, idealism, and a humanitarian nature. Negative aspects entail self-righteousness, martyrdom, and a tendency to be emotionally volatile or resentful.

Question 44: Is there a correlation or connection between an individual's birth number in numerology and their preferred music taste?

Yes, there can be some correlation between an individual's birth number in numerology and their preferred music taste. Certain traits associated with different birth numbers may align with specific music genres or styles.

For instance, people with birth numbers 1, 3, and 9 may prefer martial and inspiring tones. Those with birth numbers 2 and 7 might be more inclined towards music with string and wind instruments like violin, guitar, or flutes. Number 6 individuals may enjoy romantic and sweet music, while number 5 might seek out extremely original and unusual music. Additionally, people with birth numbers 4 and 8 may have a liking for organ or magnificent choir, or music with undertones of plaintiveness, melancholy, or religious fervour.

Question 45: How does an individual's birth number in numerology relate with their musical preferences or the type of music that resonates with them?

An individual's birth number in numerology can offer insights into their personality traits and characteristics, which in turn may influence their musical preferences or the type of music that resonates with them.

1. **Birth Number 1:** People with this birth number may be drawn to energetic and dynamic music, such as pop, rock, dance, or electronic genres. These genres mirror their lively and ambitious nature.

2. **Birth Number 2:** Those with birth number 2 might prefer soothing and melodic music, such as soft rock, acoustic ballads, or genres that emphasise harmony and emotional depth. Their sensitive and harmonious disposition aligns with such music.

3. **Birth Number 3:** Individuals with birth number 3 may enjoy music that allows for artistic expression and storytelling, like folk, country, or genres with strong lyrical content. Their creativity finds a connection in these expressive genres.

4. **Birth Number 4:** People with this birth number may appreciate music that reflects stability and structure, such as classical, jazz, or genres with a strong sense of musical arrangement and precision. The ordered and disciplined nature of these genres aligns with their personality.

5. **Birth Number 5:** Those with birth number 5 might have a diverse taste, enjoying various music genres and being open to experimentation. Their adventurous and versatile nature seeks novelty in music.

6. **Birth Number 6:** Individuals with this birth number may resonate with music that evokes emotions, like soulful ballads, romantic tunes, or genres that emphasise harmony and melodious vocals. Their nurturing and empathetic traits find solace in such music.

7. **Birth Number 7:** People with birth number 7 might be attracted to music that stimulates their mind and emotions, such as ambient, new age, classical instrumental, or genres that offer a contemplative and immersive experience. Their introspective and analytical nature finds solace in these genres.

8. **Birth Number 8:** Those with birth number 8 may appreciate music that conveys a sense of drive, motivation, or showcases strong instrumental performances, like motivational rock, energetic genres, or music with a commanding presence. Their ambitious and authoritative traits resonate with such powerful music.

9. **Birth Number 9:** Individuals with this birth number might gravitate towards music that carries emotional depth, messages of unity, or genres that emphasise social consciousness and impact. Their humanitarian and compassionate nature finds inspiration in such music.

CHAPTER 5

UNDERSTANDING THE PLANETARY CONNECTIONS

In this chapter, we embark on a cosmic voyage, exploring the profound association between numbers and planets, and how they shape our lives in remarkable ways.

Have you ever wondered if there's a number linked to every planet? Delve into the intriguing concept of numerological planetary associations and unravel the secrets of these cosmic connections.

Discover the profound influence of ruling planets in a person's numerological chart and how they can sway the tides of destiny. Explore the significance of each planet and their unique qualities, attributes, and energies that mould various aspects of our lives - be it personality traits, relationships, career paths, or spiritual growth.

As we journey through the cosmos, we'll unravel the belief that Sun represents the father and Moon, the mother, and delve into the symbolism behind the connection of fingers with specific planets. Witness how planetary energies subtly influence our moods and behaviours, and understand the challenges associated with weak planets in numerology.

And finally, we will also learn how you can make behavioural changes to align with specific planetary energies for enhanced harmony and positive outcomes in your life.

Question 46: Are there specific numbers associated with each planet?

Each planet in numerology is connected to a particular number further enhancing the significance of planetary influences.

Here are the numbers associated with each planet:

- Sun: 1

- Moon: 2

- Jupiter: 3

- Uranus: 4

- Mercury: 5

- Venus: 6

- Neptune: 7

- Saturn: 8

- Mars: 9

These numbers provide additional insights into the qualities, energies, and characteristics of each planet. By understanding the numerical associations, numerologists can delve deeper into the planetary influences in a person's birth chart and interpret their impact on various aspects of life, such as personality traits, relationships, and life events. Embracing the numerological connections to the planets allows for a more comprehensive understanding of astrological interpretations and can help guide individuals in harnessing the planetary energies for personal growth and fulfilment.

Question 47: If numerology is all about numbers, what is the connection between numbers and planets?

In numerology, there is a connection between numbers and planets, as each planet is associated with a specific number.

1. **Sun**: Sun is associated with the number 1. It represents individuality, self-expression, creativity, and leadership qualities. Sun's energy is associated with confidence, vitality, and a strong sense of identity.

2. **Moon**: Moon is associated with the number 2. It represents emotions, intuition, sensitivity, and nurturing qualities. Moon's energy is associated with empathy, adaptability, and a deep connection to one's inner self.

3. **Jupiter**: Jupiter is associated with the number 3. It represents expansion, abundance, optimism, and wisdom. Jupiter's energy is associated with growth, learning, and the pursuit of higher knowledge.

4. **Uranus**: Uranus is associated with the number 4. It represents innovation, originality, independence, and unconventional thinking. Uranus's energy is associated with sudden changes, breakthroughs, and the desire for personal freedom.

5. **Mercury**: Mercury is associated with the number 5. It represents communication, intellect, adaptability, and versatility. Mercury's energy is associated with curiosity, mental agility, and the ability to express ideas effectively.

6. **Venus**: Venus is associated with the number 6. It represents love, beauty, harmony, and relationships. Venus's energy is associated with creativity, romance, and a deep appreciation for art and aesthetics.

7. **Neptune**: Neptune is associated with the number 7. It represents spirituality, intuition, imagination, and mysticism. Neptune's energy is associated with dreams, intuition, and the exploration of the subconscious mind.

8. **Saturn**: Saturn is associated with the number 8. It represents discipline, responsibility, hard work, and material success. Saturn's energy is associated with structure, perseverance, and the lessons learned through life's challenges.

9. **Mars**: Mars is associated with the number 9. It represents action, passion, courage, and assertiveness. Mars's energy is associated with ambition, drive, and the ability to overcome obstacles.

These planetary explanations are at a basic level; relationships, connections and associations can provide additional information and interpretation when analysing numerological charts or exploring the significance of specific numbers in a person's life.

Question 48: What is the significance and influence of the ruling planet in a person's numerological chart?

The ruling planet in a person's numerological chart holds great significance as it reflects the dominant energy and qualities that shape their character and life experiences. This ruling planet provides valuable insights into their inherent talents, tendencies, and potential challenges that may arise throughout their life journey.

The influence of the ruling planet extends to various aspects of life, including personality traits, career choices, relationships, and life lessons. It governs how individuals approach life, their communication style, and their preferred ways of expressing themselves.

For example, if someone's numerological chart is ruled by Mercury, they are likely to possess strong communication skills, adaptability, and intellectual curiosity. This could lead them to excel in fields related to writing, teaching, or any profession that requires effective communication. However, they may also need to be aware of potential challenges like restlessness or overthinking.

Question 49: Are there specific remedial measures in numerology to harmonise or balance the energies of challenging planetary influences?

Yes, in numerology, there are specific remedial measures that can be undertaken to harmonise or balance the energies of challenging planetary influences. These measures aim to mitigate any negative effects and enhance the positive aspects associated with the planets.

One common remedial measure is the use of gemstones associated with specific planets. Each planet is believed to carry its own energy and vibration, and certain gemstones are associated with these planets. Wearing or keeping these gemstones close can help balance the planetary influences and promote harmony. For example, wearing a blue sapphire or an amethyst, which is associated with Saturn, or a ruby, which is associated with Sun, may help counteract challenging Saturn or Sun energies.

Additionally, performing rituals or behavioural practices related to specific planets can also help balance their energies. For instance, offering water to the rising Sun is considered a way to appease the planetary influences. Other practices might include chanting specific mantras, performing certain prayers, or engaging in acts of charity associated with a particular planet.

It's important to note that these remedial measures are not meant to change the course of destiny but rather to work in harmony with the energies present in one's numerological chart. They are intended to bring a sense of balance and peace, allowing individuals to navigate life's challenges with greater resilience and positivity.

Question 50: How can individuals make behavioural changes in order to appease planets numerologically and align themselves with the energies of specific planets for enhanced harmony and positive outcomes in their lives?

Behavioural changes to appease planets numerologically refer to the practices and actions individuals can adopt to align themselves with the energies of specific planets in their numerological chart. These changes are believed to enhance harmony and positive outcomes in different aspects of life. Here is an explanation of behavioural changes associated with appeasing planets:

1. **Sun (Surya)**: To appease the Sun, individuals may modify their behaviour by waking up early in the morning, preferably during sunrise, and offering prayers or meditating. The Sun is associated with leadership and vitality, so embracing a confident and assertive demeanour can also align with its energy.

2. **Moon (Chandra)**: Appeasing the Moon involves incorporating behaviours that promote emotional well-being and introspection. This may include setting aside time for self-reflection, maintaining a stable daily routine, and spending time in serene environments like those near water bodies or in nature.

3. **Mars (Mangal)**: To appease Mars, individuals may embrace behaviours that channel its dynamic energy positively. Engaging in regular physical exercise or sports activities can help release excessive energy and promote focus and determination.

4. **Mercury (Budha)**: Appeasing Mercury can involve behaviours that enhance mental agility and communication skills. Reading books, pursuing intellectual interests, and engaging in open and honest communication with others align with Mercury's energy.

5. **Jupiter (Guru)**: To appease Jupiter, individuals may adopt behaviours that encourage personal growth and expansion. Practising gratitude, generosity, and seeking opportunities for learning and spiritual development are ways to connect with Jupiter's energy.

6. **Venus (Shukra)**: Appeasing Venus may involve behaviours that **promote** love, beauty, and harmony. Spending quality time with loved ones, expressing affection and appreciation, and engaging in creative pursuits can resonate with Venus' energy.

7. **Saturn (Shani)**: To appease Saturn, individuals may adjust their behaviour to reflect discipline, responsibility, and perseverance. Fulfilling duties and obligations, maintaining a structured routine, and learning from challenges and setbacks can align with Saturn's energy.

Question 51: What are the qualities and attributes associated with planets in the context of numerology? How do these planetary qualities contribute to shaping various aspects of an individual's life, such as personality traits, relationships, career paths, and spiritual growth?

The qualities and attributes of planets in numerology can vary slightly depending on different interpretations and systems. However, here are some commonly associated qualities and attributes of the planets in numerology:

1. **The Sun (Surya)**: Individuality, self-expression, leadership, vitality, confidence, creativity.

2. **The Moon (Chandra)**: Emotions, intuition, nurturing, sensitivity, adaptability, receptivity.

3. **Mercury (Budha)**: Communication, intellect, flexibility, curiosity, adaptability, wit.

4. **Venus (Shukra)**: Love, beauty, harmony, romance, sensuality, aesthetics, diplomacy.

5. **Mars (Mangal)**: Energy, passion, action, assertiveness, drive, courage, ambition.

6. **Jupiter (Guru)**: Wisdom, expansion, abundance, generosity, **spirituality**, growth, optimism.

7. **Saturn (Shani)**: Responsibility, discipline, structure, perseverance, commitment, maturity.

8. **Rahu (North Node)**: Ambition, desires, illusions, cravings, unconventional thinking.

9. **Ketu (South Node)**: Spirituality, detachment, introspection, mystical experiences, karmic patterns.

Question 52: Why is it commonly believed that the Sun represents the father and the Moon represents the mother in the context of numerology?

In numerology, the belief that the Sun represents the father and the Moon represents the mother is based on ancient symbolism and archetypal associations. These representations are not meant to be taken literally, but rather as a way to understand the energies and influences that these celestial bodies embody.

Sun is often seen as the embodiment of masculine energy, reflecting the qualities typically associated with fathers. It symbolises strength, leadership, and authority. Just as the Sun provides light and direction to the world, the father is often seen as the guiding force within the family, offering protection and support. The Sun's influence in numerology is believed to shape a person's sense of identity and purpose, much like the father's role in a family's structure.

On the other hand, Moon is associated with feminine energy, embodying the qualities commonly attributed to mothers. The Moon represents nurturing, emotional depth, and intuition. Similar to how the Moon's phases affect the tides of the ocean, the mother's emotional support and care can have a profound impact on the family's emotional well-being. The Moon's energy in numerology is thought to influence a person's emotional intelligence and receptivity to the needs of others, akin to the nurturing nature of a mother.

Question 53: How are fingers of the hand connected to specific planets and what significance or symbolism does this association hold?

Fingers of the hand are believed to be connected to specific planets in numerology, each holding its significance and symbolism. That is also why it is advised that gemstones be worn on specific fingers as they are all related to different planets. Each type of gemstone has a unique connection with a particular planet, hence wearing them on the corresponding finger would enhance their beneficial effects. Here's a breakdown of this association:

1. Thumb: The thumb is linked to Mars, symbolising willpower, determination, and creative energy. It represents the ability to take action, assert oneself, and overcome challenges.

2. Index finger: The index finger is associated with Jupiter, representing wisdom, expansion, and leadership qualities. It symbolises the pursuit of knowledge, growth, and the ability to inspire and guide others.

3. Middle finger: The middle finger is connected to Saturn, representing discipline, responsibility, and the lessons we encounter in life. It symbolises patience, endurance, and the need to face and learn from life's challenges.

4. Ring finger: The ring finger is linked to the Sun, representing individuality, creativity, and personal power. It symbolises self-expression, artistic abilities, and the potential to shine brightly in one's endeavours.

5. Little finger: The little finger is associated with Mercury, representing communication, intellect, and adaptability. It symbolises the capacity for effective communication, quick thinking, and the ability to be versatile in various situations.

Question 54: How is our mood influenced by planetary energies in numerology?

In numerology, Moon's energies play a significant role in influencing our mood. As the ruler of emotions, feelings, and instincts, the Moon governs our inner world, shaping how we react emotionally to various situations. The shifting phases of the Moon can impact our mood, with the New Moon signifying new beginnings and the Full Moon amplifying emotions.

Additionally, the positions of other planets in our numerological chart can also contribute to mood fluctuations, depending on their alignment with the Moon. It's important to be aware of these planetary influences to better understand and navigate our emotional responses, promoting greater emotional balance and well-being in our lives.

Question 55: What are some symptoms or challenges associated with weak planets in numerology?

When a planet is weak in our birth chart, it can have an impact on various areas of our lives and present certain challenges. Let's explore the symptoms and challenges associated with weak planets in numerology.

A. Here are some common symptoms associated with a weak Sun:

1. **Low self-confidence**: A weak Sun can result in a lack of self-assurance and a diminished sense of self-worth. Individuals with a weak Sun may struggle to assert themselves, make decisions, or take on leadership roles confidently.

2. **Identity struggles:** The Sun represents the core identity and individuality. When weak, it can indicate difficulties in understanding one's true self and purpose in life. There may be

a lack of clarity about personal goals, passions, and a sense of direction.

3. **Lack of vitality and energy:** The Sun is associated with vitality, energy, and life force. When weak, it can contribute to low physical energy levels, fatigue, or a general lack of enthusiasm for life. Individuals may feel drained or struggle to find motivation and drive.

4. **Challenges in self-expression:** A weak Sun can manifest as difficulty expressing oneself authentically. Communication and self-expression may be inhibited, leading to challenges in asserting one's ideas, needs, and desires effectively.

5. **Limited success and recognition:** The Sun is linked to success, recognition, and achievement. When weak, it may indicate obstacles or delays in attaining recognition for one's talents and efforts. There may be a sense of unfulfilled potential or a lack of visibility in the public sphere.

6. **Father or authority issues:** The Sun represents the father figure and authority figures in one's life. A weak Sun can suggest challenges or strained relationships with the father or authority figures. There may be difficulties in establishing a healthy sense of authority and taking on leadership roles.

7. **Difficulty finding purpose:** The Sun represents one's life purpose and sense of meaning. A weak Sun can lead to a lack of clarity or confusion regarding life's purpose. Individuals may struggle to identify their passions, values, and the direction they want to pursue.

B. Here are some common symptoms associated with a weak Moon:

1. **Emotional instability:** A weak Moon can lead to heightened emotional sensitivity and instability. Individuals may experience frequent mood swings, difficulty in managing

emotions, and a tendency to be easily influenced by external circumstances.

2. **Lack of emotional nourishment:** The Moon represents nurturing and emotional well-being. When weak, it may indicate challenges in receiving emotional support or feeling a sense of inner security. There may be a longing for deeper emotional connections and a need for more nurturing in life.

3. **Unresolved past issues:** A weak Moon can bring to the surface unresolved emotional issues from the past. Individuals may struggle to let go of past hurts or traumas, leading to emotional baggage that affects their present well-being.

4. **Imbalanced intuition and instincts:** The Moon governs intuition and instincts. When weak, it may result in a lack of trust in one's instincts or difficulties in accessing and following intuitive guidance. Decision-making may be clouded, leading to confusion and indecisiveness.

5. **Sleep and mood disturbances:** The Moon is associated with sleep patterns and the subconscious mind. A weak Moon can contribute to sleep disturbances, insomnia, or vivid dreams. Mood disorders, such as depression or anxiety, may also be more prevalent.

6. **Sensitivity to environmental influences:** Individuals with a weak Moon may be more susceptible to external energies and influences. They may absorb the emotions of others easily and struggle with maintaining emotional boundaries.

7. **Challenges in nurturing and being nurtured:** A weak Moon can indicate challenges in providing nurturing and care to oneself and others. There may be difficulties in finding balance between giving and receiving support, leading to a potential imbalance in relationships.

C. Here are some common symptoms associated with a weak Jupiter:

1. **Lack of optimism and positivity:** Jupiter is known as the planet of expansion, abundance, and optimism. When weak, it can indicate a lack of optimism, a pessimistic outlook, and difficulties in maintaining a positive mindset. Individuals may struggle to see opportunities or may have a limited belief in their own potential.

2. **Limited growth and success:** Jupiter is associated with growth, success, and abundance. A weak Jupiter may result in challenges in achieving personal and professional growth. There may be limitations in career advancement, educational pursuits, or financial prosperity.

3. **Lack of confidence and self-belief:** A weak Jupiter can lead to a lack of confidence and self-belief. Individuals may doubt their abilities and may not have faith in their own potential for success. This can hinder their ability to take risks, make decisions, or seize opportunities.

4. **Difficulty in finding meaning and purpose:** Jupiter is linked to higher wisdom, spirituality, and a sense of purpose in life. When weak, individuals may struggle to find meaning and purpose. They may feel lost or unfulfilled, and there may be a lack of direction or clarity in their life path.

5. **Challenges in education and learning:** Jupiter represents knowledge, learning, and wisdom. A weak Jupiter can indicate difficulties in education, acquiring new skills, or a lack of interest in intellectual pursuits. There may be challenges in grasping complex concepts or in higher education.

6. **Excessive indulgence or lack of moderation:** Jupiter can also signify excess and indulgence. When weak, it may manifest as a lack of self-discipline and moderation. Individuals may have difficulty controlling their desires, leading to overindulgence in food, drink, or other pleasures.

7. **Lack of faith and spirituality:** Jupiter is associated with faith, belief systems, and spiritual growth. A weak Jupiter may indicate a lack of faith in higher powers or difficulty in connecting with spirituality. There may be a sense of skepticism or a disconnect from one's spiritual path.

D. Here are some common symptoms associated with a weak Rahu or Uranus:

1. **Obsessive or addictive behaviour:** A weak Rahu can lead to obsessive tendencies or addictive behaviour patterns. Individuals may struggle with excessive cravings, whether for material possessions, power, or certain experiences, leading to difficulties in finding balance and contentment.

2. **Lack of clarity and confusion:** Rahu is associated with illusions, deception, and confusion. When weak, it may indicate challenges in seeing things clearly and making sound judgments. There may be a tendency to be easily influenced by others or to get caught up in unrealistic dreams and aspirations.

3. **Lack of focus and scattered energy:** Individuals with a weak Rahu may struggle with maintaining focus and discipline. Their energy may be scattered across different pursuits and interests, making it challenging to pursue one specific path or goal with dedication.

4. **Inconsistent or unpredictable behaviour:** A weak Rahu can contribute to unpredictable behaviour and a lack of stability. Individuals may exhibit sudden mood swings, impulsive decision-making, or inconsistency in their actions, making it difficult for others to understand or rely on them.

5. **Disruption or challenges in relationships:** Rahu is known for its disruptive qualities, and when weak, it can create challenges in relationships. There may be a tendency to attract or be attracted to unconventional or unstable partners. Relationships

may experience sudden ups and downs or struggles with trust and commitment.

6. **Struggles with authority and social norms:** Individuals with a weak Rahu may rebel against authority and societal norms. They may find it challenging to conform or adhere to traditional rules and expectations, preferring to carve their own path or challenge established norms.

7. **Difficulty finding purpose or direction:** Rahu represents desires and ambitions. When weak, individuals may struggle to find their true purpose or direction in life. There may be a constant search for fulfilment, often looking for external achievements or recognition to validate their sense of self-worth.

E. Here are some common symptoms associated with a weak Mercury:

1. **Communication difficulties:** Mercury is the planet of communication and intellect. When weak, it can result in challenges in expressing oneself clearly and effectively. Individuals may struggle with articulating their thoughts, experiencing speech impediments, or difficulties in finding the right words.

2. **Learning and academic challenges:** Mercury governs intelligence, learning, and education. A weak Mercury can indicate challenges in acquiring knowledge, grasping new concepts, or performing well academically. Individuals may find it harder to concentrate, retain information, or face difficulties in exams or tests.

3. **Lack of analytical skills:** Mercury is associated with analytical thinking and problem-solving abilities. When weak, it may indicate a lack of logical reasoning, making it challenging to analyse situations or make sound decisions.

There may be a tendency to overthink or get overwhelmed by details.

4. **Memory problems:** A weak Mercury can lead to memory issues, including forgetfulness or difficulty in retaining information. Individuals may struggle to recall facts, dates, or even recent events. This can impact learning, work performance, and daily functioning.

5. **Lack of adaptability:** Mercury represents adaptability and flexibility. When weak, individuals may find it challenging to adapt to new environments, changes, or different perspectives. There may be a resistance to change, rigidity in thinking, or difficulty in adjusting to new situations.

6. **Miscommunication and misunderstandings:** With a weak Mercury, there may be a higher likelihood of miscommunication and misunderstandings in personal and professional relationships. Individuals may struggle to convey their thoughts accurately, leading to confusion or conflicts in communication.

7. **Challenges in business and financial matters:** Mercury is also associated with business acumen and financial matters. When weak, individuals may face difficulties in business ventures, financial planning, or managing finances effectively. There may be challenges in negotiation skills or making strategic decisions.

F. Here are some common symptoms associated with a weak Venus:

1. **Difficulty in establishing and maintaining harmonious relationships:** Venus is the planet of love, relationships, and harmony. When weak, it may indicate challenges in forming and sustaining healthy, balanced relationships. There may be issues with finding emotional fulfilment, attracting compatible partners, or maintaining harmony in existing relationships.

2. **Lack of appreciation for beauty and aesthetics:** Venus represents beauty, art, and aesthetics. A weak Venus can lead to a diminished appreciation for art, music, and the finer things in life. Individuals may struggle to find joy and pleasure in artistic pursuits or have a limited sense of style and fashion.

3. **Low self-esteem and self-worth:** Venus governs self-esteem, self-worth, and self-love. When weak, it can result in a lack of confidence in one's own attractiveness and value. Individuals may struggle with feelings of inadequacy, seeking external validation, or experience difficulty in accepting love and affection from others.

4. **Challenges in finding and experiencing romantic love:** A weak Venus can indicate difficulties in finding and experiencing romantic love. There may be obstacles in attracting and forming romantic partnerships, or relationships may lack depth, passion, or long-term fulfilment.

5. **Financial instability or overspending:** Venus is associated with material abundance and financial prosperity. When weak, it may lead to challenges in financial matters. Individuals may struggle with financial instability, overspend on luxury items, or face difficulties in managing finances effectively.

6. **Imbalance in giving and receiving love:** Venus represents the balance between giving and receiving love and affection. When weak, there may be an imbalance in this dynamic. Individuals may struggle with either giving too much and not receiving in return, or receiving love without being able to reciprocate.

7. **Lack of artistic expression or creativity:** Venus is linked to artistic expression and creativity. A weak Venus can result in challenges in expressing artistic talents or finding creative inspiration. Individuals may struggle to tap into their artistic potential or feel blocked in their creative endeavours.

G. Here are some symptoms or challenges associated with a weak Ketu or Neptune:

1. **Lack of spiritual connection:** Ketu or Neptune represents spirituality, enlightenment, and detachment. When weak, individuals may struggle to establish a deep spiritual connection or find meaning in spiritual practices. There may be a sense of detachment from higher realms of consciousness.

2. **Confusion and lack of clarity:** A weak Ketu can manifest as confusion and a lack of clarity in one's life path and goals. Individuals may find it challenging to discern their true purpose or feel uncertain about their direction in life. Decision-making may be clouded, leading to a sense of being lost.

3. **Inability to let go of the past:** Ketu is associated with letting go and releasing attachments. When weak, individuals may have difficulty moving on from past experiences or letting go of old patterns and beliefs. This can hinder personal growth and prevent them from embracing new opportunities.

4. **Tendency towards escapism:** A weak Ketu can lead to a tendency towards escapism or avoidance of reality. Individuals may seek distractions or engage in addictive behaviours as a way to escape emotional or psychological challenges. There may be a resistance to facing the deeper aspects of oneself.

5. **Struggles with selflessness and empathy:** Ketu represents selflessness and universal compassion. When weak, individuals may find it challenging to express empathy towards others or prioritise the needs of others above their own. There may be a tendency towards self-centeredness or a lack of understanding of collective welfare.

6. **Illusions and confusion:** When weak, it can lead to confusion, delusions, and a blurred sense of reality. Individuals may struggle with distinguishing truth from fantasy and may be prone to escapism through daydreaming or fantasy.

7. **Lack of boundaries:** Neptune represents the dissolution of boundaries and merging with the collective. When weak, individuals may struggle with establishing healthy boundaries in relationships, leading to a tendency to be easily influenced or manipulated. There may be challenges in maintaining personal identity and autonomy.

8. **Addictive tendencies:** A weak Neptune can contribute to addictive tendencies and substance abuse issues. Individuals may seek to escape reality through addictive behaviours or substances as a way to cope with emotional or psychological challenges. There may be a vulnerability to deception and susceptibility to negative influences.

9. **Creative blocks:** Neptune governs creativity, inspiration, and artistic expression. When weak, individuals may experience creative blocks or difficulties tapping into their creative potential. There may be challenges in finding inspiration or bringing creative ideas to fruition.

H. Here are some common symptoms associated with a weak Saturn:

1. **Lack of discipline and structure:** Saturn represents discipline, responsibility, and structure. When weak, individuals may struggle with maintaining discipline and adhering to routines. There may be difficulties in organising tasks, meeting deadlines, or establishing a sense of structure in daily life.

2. **Low self-esteem and self-confidence:** A weak Saturn can result in low self-esteem and self-confidence. Individuals may doubt their abilities, feel inadequate, or experience a lack of self-belief. This can lead to self-imposed limitations and a fear of taking on new challenges or responsibilities.

3. **Challenges in career and professional life:** Saturn governs career, ambition, and achievement. When weak, it can indicate challenges or delays in career progression. Individuals may

face obstacles in their professional life, experience setbacks, or struggle to find fulfilment and success in their chosen field.

4. **Difficulty in handling responsibilities:** Saturn represents responsibilities and obligations. When weak, individuals may find it challenging to handle responsibilities effectively. There may be a tendency to procrastinate, avoidance in taking on leadership roles, or struggle with a sense of overwhelm when faced with obligations.

5. **Lack of patience and perseverance:** Saturn is associated with patience, endurance, and perseverance. A weak Saturn can indicate a lack of patience and a tendency to give up easily. Individuals may find it difficult to stay committed to long-term goals or persist through challenges and obstacles.

6. **Fear and anxiety:** Saturn is often associated with fears and restrictions. When weak, individuals may experience heightened anxiety, worry, or a sense of insecurity. There may be a fear of failure, criticism, or a reluctance to take risks due to a fear of the unknown.

7. **Difficulty in forming and maintaining relationships:** Saturn also represents relationships and commitments. When weak, individuals may experience challenges in forming and maintaining stable, long-lasting relationships. There may be difficulties in establishing emotional connections, fear of intimacy, or a tendency to prioritize personal goals over relationships.

I. Here are some common symptoms associated with a weak Mars:

1. **Low energy and lack of motivation:** Mars is the planet of energy, drive, and motivation. When weak, individuals may experience a lack of physical and mental energy. They may struggle with finding motivation to take action, initiating tasks, or pursuing goals.

2. **Lack of assertiveness and confidence:** Mars represents assertiveness, courage, and self-confidence. A weak Mars can result in a lack of assertiveness and difficulty standing up for oneself. Individuals may lack self-confidence, feel passive, or struggle with self-assertion.

3. **Indecisiveness and lack of initiative:** Mars is associated with decisiveness and taking initiative. When weak, individuals may experience indecisiveness, hesitancy, or a tendency to procrastinate. They may struggle with making choices and taking the necessary steps to move forward.

4. **Conflict and aggression issues:** Mars is the planet of aggression and assertion. When weak, it can lead to challenges in managing anger and conflicts. Individuals may have difficulty expressing their anger constructively or may suppress it, leading to pent-up frustration or passive-aggressive behaviour.

5. **Reduced physical strength and vitality:** Mars governs physical strength, vitality, and stamina. A weak Mars can indicate a lack of physical endurance, and reduced vitality. Individuals may experience lower resistance to illness, get fatigued easily, or struggle with physical activities.

6. **Lack of focus and direction:** Mars is associated with focus, determination, and goal-oriented behaviour. When weak, individuals may struggle with maintaining focus and direction in their pursuits. They may find it challenging to stay committed to long-term goals or lack clarity in their objectives.

7. **Relationship and intimacy issues:** Mars also governs passion and sexual energy. When weak, individuals may experience challenges in intimate relationships. They may struggle with expressing their desires or have a reduced libido. There may be difficulties in cultivating a fulfilling and passionate love life.

CHAPTER 6

NURTURING BALANCE AND ALIGNMENT THROUGH ZODIAC SIGNS AND ELEMENTS

In this captivating chapter, we will unravel the mysteries of the stars and how they influence our lives, offering profound insights into our personalities, emotions, and paths to personal growth.

Ever wondered about the significance of zodiac signs and how to explore their wisdom? Discover the secrets of each zodiac sign and how they hold the keys to self-discovery.

Delve into the intriguing difference between Sun Signs and Moon Signs and how these luminaries shape our unique characteristics and emotional landscapes.

Unlock the power of the three modalities of zodiac signs - cardinal, fixed, and mutable, and learn how understanding these concepts can enhance your self-awareness and personal development.

As we journey further, we'll explore how zodiac signs are divided into elements and the profound significance this elemental division holds. Unravel the elemental characteristics commonly associated with zodiac signs and witness how they contribute to our creativity, intuition, practicality, and emotional depth.

At the end, peek into the fascinating world of numerological symbolism, where fingers are associated with elements, and each finger holds a unique and profound meaning.

Question 56: What are Zodiac Signs? How can I learn about them?

Zodiac signs are a set of 12 astrological signs that are believed to reflect different personality traits and characteristics of individuals based on their birth dates. These signs are Aries, Taurus, Gemini, Cancer, Leo, Virgo, Libra, Scorpio, Sagittarius, Capricorn, Aquarius, and Pisces. Each sign is associated with specific elements and ruled by different planets.

The zodiac signs can be grouped into four divisions based on the elements they represent: Fire, Water, Air, and Earth. Each division consists of three signs.

The Fire Triangle:

1st House – March 21st to April 19th

2nd House – July 21st to August 20th

3rd House – November 21st to December 20th

The Water Triangle:

1st House – June 21st to July 20th

2nd House – October 21st to November 20th

3rd House – February 19th to March 20th

The Air Triangle:

1st House – May 21st to June 20th

2nd House – September 21st to October 20th

3rd House – January 21st to February 19th

The Earth Triangle:

1st House – April 21st to May 20th

2nd House – August 21st to September 20th

3rd House – December 21st to January 20th

Question 57: What is the difference between Sun Sign and Moon Sign?

The Sun Sign and Moon Sign are two important components of an individual's astrological chart, each representing different aspects of their personality. The Sun Sign signifies the core identity, behaviour, ego, and overall outlook on life. It is determined by the position of the Sun at the time of birth and is associated with the traditional zodiac sign corresponding to the birthdate. Understanding your Sun Sign can give you insights into your conscious self, how you express yourself to the world, and your fundamental characteristics.

On the other hand, Moon Sign represents the emotional nature, instincts, intuition, and subconscious tendencies of a person. It is determined by the position of the Moon at the precise date, time, and location of birth. Moon Sign delves into the inner realm of emotions and sheds light on your emotional responses, unconscious patterns, and intuitive inclinations. Understanding your Moon Sign can help you become more aware of your emotional needs, how you process feelings, and what brings you a sense of security and comfort.

By considering both your Sun Sign and Moon Sign, you can gain a more comprehensive understanding of yourself. Integrating the qualities of both signs can provide valuable insights into your personality, relationships, and life journey. Exploring your Sun Sign and Moon Sign can help you embrace your strengths, navigate challenges, and align with your authentic self.

Question 58: What are the three modalities of the zodiac signs?

The three modalities of the zodiac signs are cardinal, fixed, and mutable. These modalities indicate different energy and behaviour styles exhibited by the signs.

Question 59: In the context of numerology, what do the terms cardinal, fixed, and mutable signs represent, and how can understanding these concepts enhance self-awareness and personal development?

In numerology, the terms cardinal, fixed, and mutable signs are related to the twelve zodiac signs and can offer valuable insights into our personalities and behaviour, thus enhancing self-awareness and personal development. Here's a brief explanation of how these concepts can contribute to personal growth:

1. **Cardinal Signs:** Cardinal signs are Aries, Cancer, Libra, and Capricorn. They represent initiation, leadership, and assertiveness. Understanding cardinal energy can help you recognize your ability to take charge, initiate new projects, and display determination. Embracing this energy empowers you to develop leadership qualities and assert your desires, leading to personal growth and the pursuit of your goals.

2. **Fixed Signs:** Taurus, Leo, Scorpio, and Aquarius are the fixed signs associated with determination, endurance, and stability. Recognizing fixed energy helps you understand your strengths in maintaining stability, persisting through challenges, and staying committed to your endeavours. Embracing this energy fosters reliability, loyalty, and the ability to stay focused on long-term goals.

3. **Mutable Signs:** Gemini, Virgo, Sagittarius, and Pisces are the mutable signs representing adaptability, flexibility, and versatility. Understanding mutable energy assists you in navigating change, transitions, and various circumstances with ease. Embracing this energy encourages open-mindedness, resourcefulness, and the ability to adjust to new situations, fostering personal growth and a willingness to explore different perspectives.

By understanding these concepts and reflecting on how they manifest in your life, you can gain valuable self-awareness. Recognizing and embracing these qualities within yourself can help you harness your strengths, address your weaknesses, and cultivate a more balanced and fulfilling life. It's essential to remember that personal development is a multidimensional process, and incorporating various frameworks and approaches can provide a holistic understanding of oneself. So, whether it's numerology or astrology, exploring these concepts can be beneficial for personal growth and self-improvement.

Question 60: What is the significance of dividing zodiac signs into elements, and how does this elemental division help in understanding the unique characteristics and dynamics of each zodiac sign?

Zodiac signs are indeed divided into elements. There are four elements: fire, earth, air, and water. Each zodiac sign is associated with one of these elements, which influences their overall energy, characteristics, and behaviour.

Here is the breakdown of zodiac signs and their corresponding elements:

1. **Fire Signs:** Aries, Leo, Sagittarius

2. **Earth Signs:** Taurus, Virgo, Capricorn

3. **Air Signs:** Gemini, Libra, Aquarius

4. **Water Signs:** Cancer, Scorpio, Pisces

Question 61: What are the elemental characteristics that are commonly associated with zodiac signs in numerology, and how do these elements contribute to an individual's expression of creativity, practicality, intuition, or emotional depth?

In numerology, zodiac signs are commonly associated with specific elements, each contributing to different aspects of an individual's personality and expression. These elemental characteristics offer insights into how people interact with the world and approach various aspects of life.

1. **Fire Signs: Aries, Leo, Sagittarius**

    Fire signs possess a fiery and passionate nature fuelling their creativity and zest for life. They are natural leaders and are often driven by their creative pursuits. Their dynamic energy and enthusiasm make them inspirational to others.

2. **Earth Signs: Taurus, Virgo, Capricorn**

    Earth signs are grounded, practical, and reliable. They approach life with a down-to-earth attitude and excel in managing practical matters. Their creativity is expressed through their ability to bring ideas to tangible reality.

3. **Air Signs: Gemini, Libra, Aquarius**

    Air signs are intellectual and social beings, with strong communication skills. Their creativity lies in their ability to generate innovative ideas and find solutions to complex problems. They excel in creative pursuits involving communication, arts, and networking.

4. Water Signs: Cancer, Scorpio, Pisces

Water signs are emotionally deep, intuitive, and empathetic. Their creativity is driven by their emotional connection and profound understanding of human feelings. They excel in artistic and spiritual expressions, often tapping into their subconscious for inspiration.

Question 62: How are fingers associated with elements and what symbolic meanings are attributed to each finger?

The fingers hold special significance as they are associated with the four elements - fire, air, earth, and water. Each finger symbolises different traits and energies based on these elemental associations.

1. **Thumb (Fire):** The thumb is linked with the element of fire. Fire represents passion, determination, and action. The thumb is believed to reflect a person's willpower, and their ability to be decisive and take action in life.

2. **Index Finger (Air):** The index finger corresponds to the element of air. Air is connected to intellect, communication, and ideas. The index finger represents attributes like ambition and the ability to effectively express oneself.

3. **Middle Finger (Ether/Spirit):** The middle finger is sometimes associated with the element of ether or spirit. Ether is considered the fifth element in certain esoteric traditions and represents higher consciousness. The middle finger is believed to symbolise responsibility, discipline, and a connection to one's spiritual nature.

4. **Ring Finger (Earth):** The ring finger is linked to the element of earth. Earth represents stability, practicality, and grounding. The ring finger is associated with qualities like creativity and practicality. It also reflects aspects of one's relationships and their ability to maintain harmony and balance in life.

5. **Little Finger (Water):** The little finger is associated with the element of water. Water represents emotions, intuition, and adaptability. The little finger is believed to represent communication skills, social interactions, and emotional expression.

CHAPTER 7

NUMEROLOGY AND COMPATIBILITY: UNLOCKING THE POTENTIAL OF YOUR RELATIONSHIPS

Love and relationships- the essence of life's journey- are as enchanting as they are complex. Have you ever wondered how numerology can shed light on your relationship dynamics?

Discover how numerology holds the key to improving your relationships. Unravel the fascinating insights it provides about the challenges and dynamics of relationships when partners' numerological numbers are not compatible. How does this influence the journey of love, and what are the factors that can make or break a relationship?

The choice of a wedding date is more than just a date on a calendar. Numerology bestows a unique advantage in choosing a wedding date that aligns with the couple's energies, setting the stage for a harmonious and blissful marital journey. Explore how this mystical practice can shape your relationship's destiny.

Dive into the captivating exploration of elemental associations in numerology and how they play a vital role in assessing compatibility between individuals. Discover the profound significance of elemental factors in creating a balanced and harmonious relationship.

Question 63: How can numerology help me improve my relationships?

Numerology offers valuable insights into improving relationships by analysing the numbers associated with you and your partner. It delves into the characteristics, behaviours, health issues, challenges, strengths, and weaknesses of both individuals. Numerology also examines the impact of names, signatures, mobile phone vibrations, and compatibility of individual numbers and elements.

By understanding each other's numerological profiles and reports, you gain a deeper understanding of yourselves and your partner. This knowledge allows you to follow suggestions tailored to your unique numerical influences. It helps improve communication, identify areas of compatibility, and potential conflicts. With this awareness, you can work together towards building a stronger and fulfilling relationship.

Numerology acts as a guide, highlighting the dynamics at play within the relationship. It fosters empathy, understanding, and acceptance of each other's differences. By embracing the insights provided by numerology, you can create a harmonious and supportive bond, nurturing love, trust, and mutual growth.

Remember, numerology is just one tool to enhance relationships. It should be combined with open communication, respect, and a willingness to invest time and effort into the partnership. Use numerology as a catalyst for self-awareness and as a stepping stone towards deeper connections with your loved ones.

Question 64: What insights can numerology provide about the potential challenges and dynamics of a relationship when the numerological numbers of partners are incompatible, and how does it influence the likelihood of relationship success or failure?

Numerology can provide insights into the potential challenges and dynamics of a relationship when the numerological numbers of partners are incompatible. However, it is important to note that numerology does not determine the definitive success or failure of a relationship. It serves as a tool for understanding and navigating the dynamics between partners, and provides solutions by making changes in spelling of names, signatures and few other corrective measures.

Numerology considers various factors, such as birth numbers, birth dates, elements, marriage dates, and personal years of both partners, to assess their compatibility. Incompatibility may indicate differences in personality traits, life goals, or communication styles, which can lead to challenges within the relationship.

Numerology identifies specific areas where conflicts or differences might arise between partners. It highlights potential obstacles or contrasting approaches to life, indicating areas that may require more understanding, compromise, and effective communication.

However, successful relationships are not solely determined by numerological compatibility. The success of a relationship depends on the individuals involved and their willingness to work through challenges, communicate openly, and cultivate a strong emotional connection.

Numerology can serve as a guide for self-awareness and personal growth within the relationship. Understanding one's numerological profile allows individuals to recognize their strengths, weaknesses, and areas for improvement. This self-awareness can foster personal development and contribute to the overall dynamics of the relationship.

Ultimately, the likelihood of a relationship's success or failure is influenced by the commitment, effort, and compatibility between partners, both on a numerological level and in other aspects of their connection. Effective communication, willingness to adapt, mutual respect, and shared values are crucial ingredients for a thriving relationship, regardless of numerological compatibility.

Question 65: What are the benefits of selecting a wedding date based on numerology, and how can it impact the couple's marital journey and relationship dynamics?

1. **Positive Energies:** Choosing a wedding date that aligns harmoniously with the couple's numerological profiles can attract positive energies to the ceremony and marriage. This fosters a harmonious and supportive environment, laying a strong foundation for their marital journey.

2. **Enhanced Compatibility:** Numerology can assess the compatibility between the couple's birth dates, offering insights into their compatibility as partners. By selecting a wedding date that aligns well with both individuals' numerological profiles, the couple can enhance overall compatibility, increasing the likelihood of a harmonious and fulfilling marriage. Synchronising the energies of the wedding date with the couple's individual numerological vibrations can contribute to a more balanced and supportive relationship.

Question 66: How does numerology assess the compatibility between individuals by considering their elemental associations, and what role do these elemental factors play in determining a harmonious and balanced relationship?

In numerology, assessing the compatibility between individuals goes beyond just the numbers derived from their names and birthdates. It also involves considering the elemental associations linked to their birthdates. These elemental factors play a significant role in determining the overall harmony and balance in a relationship.

Let's look at some examples of how elemental compatibility works in numerology:

1. **Fire and Water:** Fire and Water elements can sometimes clash due to their contrasting natures. Fire is assertive, passionate, and energetic, while Water is sensitive, emotional, and intuitive. In a relationship, Fire's intense nature may overwhelm Water's gentle sensitivity, leading to conflicts and misunderstandings. However, when these elements find a way to balance and support each other, their relationship can be passionate, nurturing, and transformative.

2. **Earth and Water:** Earth and Water elements often create a strong and nurturing compatibility. Earth is practical, stable, and grounded, while Water is emotional, intuitive, and empathetic. In a relationship, Earth provides a solid foundation and a sense of security, allowing Water to express their emotions freely. Water, in turn, brings depth and understanding to the relationship. Together, they create a safe and supportive environment for each other.

3. **Fire and Air:** Fire and Air elements tend to have an exciting and stimulating compatibility. Fire is passionate, energetic, and creative, while Air is intellectual, communicative, and curious. In a relationship, Fire and Air inspire each other, leading to dynamic conversations, shared adventures, and a strong sense of camaraderie. Fire encourages Air's creativity, while Air helps Fire articulate their ideas and emotions. However, finding the right balance between Air and Fire is crucial. Too much Air in relation to Fire can dilute Fire's intensity, making it harder for Fire to sustain its vitality. On the other hand, too little Air may hinder Fire's ability to ignite or maintain its fiery energy. Therefore, it's essential for Fire and Air to strike a harmonious equilibrium to thrive in their relationship.

CHAPTER 8

EXPLORING NUMEROLOGY'S CONNECTION WITH HEALTH & WELLBEING

Your well-being is your most precious asset. Have you ever wondered how numerology can play a role in understanding and improving your health and lifestyle?

Discover how numerology holds the potential to offer valuable insights into your overall health and well-being. Uncover the ways in which numerology can impact your lifestyle choices, leading to a path of greater balance and harmony.

Explore the mystical aspects of numerology that can shed light on potential health challenges and guide you towards optimal lifestyle decisions. From identifying health vulnerabilities to determining the most suitable dietary guidelines based on your birth number, numerology is brimming with secrets that can enhance your vitality and longevity.

Question 67: Can numerology provide insights into my health and well-being?

Numerology offers insights into understanding health and wellness by examining various numerological factors such as birth number, destiny number, and more. It provides valuable information about both physical and emotional well-being.

Through numerology, you can identify potential areas of concern regarding your health. By understanding the numerical influences, you become more alert and vigilant about taking proactive measures to maintain optimal health. Numerology acts as a guiding tool, helping you recognize potential health issues and take necessary precautions.

Numerology encourages a holistic approach to wellness. It prompts you to pay attention to both your physical and emotional well-being. By understanding the numerical vibrations associated with your health, you can make informed choices about your lifestyle, diet, exercise, and self-care routines.

While numerology can offer valuable insights, it is important to note that it is not a substitute for professional medical advice. It should be used as a complementary tool in conjunction with proper medical care and consultation. By combining numerological guidance with medical expertise, you can take proactive steps towards maintaining your health and overall well-being.

Question 68: How can Numerology impact lifestyle?

Numerology has the potential to greatly impact and influence lifestyle changes by providing valuable insights, guidance, and a deeper understanding of oneself. Here are some ways in which numerology can have an impact:

1. **Self-awareness:** Numerology helps individuals gain a better understanding of their personality traits, strengths, weaknesses, and life patterns. This self-awareness forms a solid foundation

for making conscious lifestyle choices that align with their authentic selves. It offers guidance and clarity when considering important aspects such as career choices, relationships, or overall life goals.

2. **Personal Year Number:** The Personal Year Number in numerology reveals the themes and opportunities that will be present during a specific year. By knowing their Personal Year Number, individuals can align their lifestyle choices with the energies and lessons of that year. This empowers them to make conscious decisions that support their personal growth and development.

3. **Compatibility:** Numerology provides insights into compatibility with others, whether it's in personal relationships, friendships, or business partnerships. By considering numerological compatibility, individuals can make informed decisions about their social connections. This understanding can have a significant impact on their lifestyle and overall well-being.

4. **Balanced Living:** Numerology encourages individuals to find balance and harmony in various areas of life. It offers insights into areas that may need attention or improvement, such as work-life balance, relationships, health, or spirituality. By understanding the numerical influences at play, individuals can make necessary adjustments to create a more balanced and fulfilling lifestyle.

5. **Timing and Decision-Making:** Numerology can be a helpful tool when it comes to timing important lifestyle changes. By understanding the cycles and patterns associated with specific numbers, individuals can make well-timed decisions and initiate changes at opportune moments. This maximises their chances for success and personal growth.

6. **Personal Growth and Transformation:** Numerology provides a framework for personal growth and transformation. It guides individuals in identifying areas for self-improvement,

overcoming challenges, and embracing new opportunities. By integrating numerological insights into their lifestyle choices, individuals can facilitate positive change and personal development.

Overall, numerology offers valuable tools and perspectives that can significantly impact an individual's lifestyle. It provides guidance, self-awareness, and a deeper understanding of oneself, enabling individuals to make informed decisions, embrace personal growth, and create a more balanced and fulfilling life.

Question 69: Can numerology provide insights into health and well-being, such as identifying potential health challenges or determining optimal lifestyle choices?

Numerology can indeed provide insights into health and well-being by examining the numerical vibrations associated with an individual's birth date, name, or other relevant factors. While it is not a substitute for professional medical advice, numerology can offer unique perspectives and highlight potential patterns or tendencies that may be relevant to one's health.

For example, let's consider the influence of numbers on health indications:

- If your birth date adds up to 1 (e.g., born on the 1st, 10th, 19th, or 28th), you may have a tendency to experience early eye problems, blood pressure issues, or palpitations.

- Those born on dates adding up to 2 (e.g., 2nd, 11th, 20th, 29th) may have a predisposition to digestive issues or stomach problems.

- Individuals born on dates totalling to 3 (e.g., 3rs, 12th, 21st, 30th) may be prone to conditions such as sciatica or skin issues.

- If your birth date reduces to 4 (e.g., 4th, 13th, 22nd, 31st), you may have a tendency to experience headaches or back pain.

- Those with a birth date adding up to 5 (e.g., 5th, 14th, 23rd) may be more susceptible to insomnia or nervous system-related issues.

- If your birth date reduces to 6 (e.g., 6th, 15th, 24th), you may have a tendency to throat, chest, or breast-related issues.

- Individuals born on dates totalling 7 (e.g., 7th, 16th, 25th) may be prone to sensitive skin issues or nervousness.

- If your birth date adds up to 8 (e.g., 8th, 17th, 26th), you might have a tendency to experience liver problems or issues related to gas.

- Those born on dates totalling 9 (e.g., 9th, 18th, 27th) may have a tendency to fever or being accident-prone.

While these examples highlight potential associations between numbers and health, it is crucial to remember that numerology should be considered in conjunction with professional medical advice and other aspects of maintaining well-being. Numerology serves as an additional tool to enhance self-awareness, encourage proactive health measures, and guide individuals towards making optimal lifestyle choices.

Question 70: What are some recommended dietary guidelines based on one's birth number in numerology?

Based on one's birth number, certain dietary guidelines can be suggested to support and enhance the individual's inherent qualities and characteristics. Here are some recommended dietary guidelines for each birth number:

1. **Birth Number 1:** Individuals with birth number 1 are often known for their vitality and leadership qualities. To support their active lifestyle and boost their energy, they are advised to include protein-rich foods like lean meats, fish, eggs, peas, lentils, cottage cheese and legumes. Brain health is crucial for

their sharp thinking, so incorporating nuts, seeds, saffron, cloves, raisins, bay leaf, orange, and lemon can be beneficial.

2. **Birth Number 2:** People with birth number 2 are known for their harmonious and balanced nature. For emotional well-being and hormonal balance, they should focus on a diet that includes whole grains, fruits, and vegetables. Foods like flaxseeds and soy products, lettuce, cabbage, cucumber, and melons can help maintain hormonal equilibrium.

3. **Birth Number 3:** Those with birth number 3 are often creative and expressive. To enhance their creativity and communication skills, they are encouraged to include a variety of colourful fruits and vegetables, along with beets, strawberries, pomegranates, pineapples, grapes, saffron, nutmeg, and cloves. Foods like honey and herbal teas can also support their ability to communicate effectively.

4. **Birth Number 4:** Individuals with birth number 4 are practical and grounded. Their diet should focus on stability and body support, including whole grains, lean proteins, spinach, fruits, and vegetables. Foods rich in calcium, like dairy products and leafy greens, can also contribute to their overall well-being.

5. **Birth Number 5:** People with birth number 5 are adventurous and dynamic. They should include a variety of fruits, vegetables, whole grains, oats, lean proteins, and healthy fats in their diet to match their active lifestyle. Brain-boosting foods like berries, walnuts, hazelnuts, and omega-3 rich fish can also be beneficial.

6. **Birth Number 6:** Those with birth number 6 are nurturing and caring. They are advised to include fresh fruits, vegetables, whole grains, lean proteins, and dairy products in their diet. Foods that support digestion and balance, such as fermented foods and herbal teas, can further enhance their caring nature.

7. **Birth Number 7:** Individuals with birth number 7 are introspective and spiritual. Their diet should focus on fresh fruits, vegetables, whole grains, lettuce, cucumber, cabbage,

mushrooms, apples, grapes, juices, and plant-based proteins. Nuts and seeds can enhance their mental clarity and focus.

8. **Birth Number 8:** People with birth number 8 seek abundance and success. They should include foods that provide sustained energy, such as complex carbohydrates and healthy fats. Foods like leafy greens, spinach, carrots, and cruciferous vegetables can support their liver and digestive system.

9. **Birth Number 9:** Those with birth number 9 are compassionate and humanitarian. Their diet should be rich in fruits, vegetables, onions, garlic, ginger, pepper, whole grains, and plant-based proteins. Foods like leafy greens and herbal teas can help detoxify and cleanse their bodies.

It's important to remember that these are general guidelines, and individual dietary needs may vary based on factors such as age, activity level, and health conditions. Consulting a healthcare professional or registered dietician is always recommended for personalised nutritional advice that meets individual needs and health goals.

CHAPTER 9

HARNESSING NUMEROLOGY FOR FINANCIAL ABUNDANCE

Have you ever wondered if there's a secret code in numbers that could unlock the doors to financial prosperity? In this chapter, we will unravel the fascinating ways in which numerology can be harnessed to enhance your financial opportunities and increase prosperity in your life. From guiding you in making wise financial choices to empowering your entrepreneurial ventures, numerology offers insights that could lead to greater success and growth.

Discover the significance of using a "lucky" brand name for your business or product, and how it can impact your business's performance. If you've ever questioned whether changing your business's name could be the solution to a struggling venture, we'll explore the potential benefits and considerations in doing so.

Question 71: How can numerology assist me in making financial decisions?

Numerology can be a valuable tool in guiding your financial decisions. By examining your birth numbers, numerology provides insights into various aspects of your finances. It reveals information about opportunities, potential delays, luck factors, and obstacles that may come your way.

Numerology sheds light on whether you are better suited for business or service-oriented endeavours. It identifies which numbers are more financially auspicious for you and suggests lines of work that align with your individual numbers and elements.

By considering all this information, numerology empowers you to make more informed financial decisions. It provides a deeper understanding of your financial strengths and weaknesses, allowing you to navigate potential risks and seize opportunities that align with your numerical influences.

However, it is important to note that numerology is just one aspect to consider when making financial decisions. It should be used alongside other factors, such as practical considerations, market research, and professional financial advice. Numerology acts as a guiding tool to enhance your financial awareness and decision-making, but ultimately, the final choices are in your hands.

Question 72: How can numerology be used to enhance financial opportunities and increase prosperity in one's life?

Numerology offers valuable insights into financial opportunities and prosperity by examining personal numbers like birth number, destiny number, and personal year. These numbers reveal innate talents and strengths, guiding individuals towards career paths and financial endeavours that align with their natural abilities, increasing the likelihood of success.

Moreover, numerology recognizes the cyclic nature of life. By calculating the Personal Year Number, individuals can identify favourable periods for financial growth and seize opportunities during these times, whether in investments, career changes, or business ventures.

Additionally, numerology can be applied to business names and branding. Selecting a name with numerological compatibility can attract positive energies, enhancing the prospects for financial success. It is believed that harmonising the numerological vibrations of your name and your business name can create a more favourable environment for wealth creation.

Question 73: How can numerology be utilised to improve business performance and increase success in entrepreneurial endeavours?

Numerology offers valuable insights to enhance business performance and increase success in entrepreneurial endeavours. By analysing the energy and vibrations associated with the business name, one can attract positive energies and improve the likelihood of success. A name that aligns well with favourable numerological numbers can create a strong brand identity and attract more customers and clients.

1. **Numerological Compatibility:** Numerology also helps assess the compatibility between individuals involved in the business, such as business partners or key stakeholders. Understanding the numerological dynamics and potential challenges between individuals allows you to establish effective communication, collaboration, and harmony within the business. This fosters a positive work environment and maximises productivity, enabling the business to thrive.

2. **Business Logo and Branding:** Applying numerology to the design and symbolism of your business logo and branding further strengthens your brand identity. By incorporating numerologically harmonious elements into your visual identity, you can create a powerful and resonant brand image. This attracts customers and aligns with the essence of your business, making it more appealing to your target audience.

3. **Personal Numerological Traits:** As an entrepreneur, gaining insights into your personal numerological traits, such as Birth

Number or Destiny Number, can be extremely beneficial. Understanding your inherent strengths and areas for growth empowers you to make informed decisions that align with your natural abilities. By leveraging your strengths and addressing potential challenges, you can optimise your performance as a business leader and increase your chances of success.

Question 74: What is the significance and potential benefits of using a "lucky" brand name for a business or product?

A "lucky" brand name holds significant potential benefits for a business or product. Such a name can create positive associations in the minds of customers, evoking feelings of trust, positivity, and good fortune. When people perceive a name as lucky or auspicious, it can attract more customers and enhance the brand's image.

However, it's important to remember that a lucky brand name is just one piece of the puzzle in building a successful brand. Other crucial factors like product quality, excellent customer service, effective marketing strategies, and overall brand experience also contribute to the business' success. A lucky brand name can serve as a positive starting point, but it must be complemented by a strong brand identity and a commitment to delivering value to customers. The combination of a lucky name with these essential elements can significantly boost the business' prospects and make it more appealing to potential customers.

Question 75: If my business is not doing well, should I consider changing its name as a potential solution for improvement?

If your current business name is not connecting well with your intended customers or is holding back your business growth, then changing the name could be a possible solution worth exploring. A new name that is more auspicious and lucky, with positive vibrations and is in sync with you own numbers, which also resonates with your target market and reflects your products or services, can help reinvigorate your brand and attract fresh customers.

However, it's essential to remember that a name change alone won't magically fix all problems. Take a holistic approach to assess your business thoroughly. Evaluate your products or services, marketing strategies, target audience, and overall business strategy. Ensure that the change in name aligns with your numerological preferences and complements the direction you want your business to take.

CHAPTER 10

UNVEILING THE HIDDEN MEANING OF MOBILE, HOUSE, AND VEHICLE NUMBERS

In the world of numerology, even the numbers of our mobile, house, and vehicle can play a role in shaping our destiny. In this chapter, we will explore how mobile numbers carry a special importance in numerology and the process of calculating their numerological significance.

House numbers also hold a significant place in numerology, and we will unravel their importance and the impact they can have on our lives. If you've ever questioned whether an unlucky house number can be a cause for concern, we will delve into the considerations and potential solutions.

And that's not all – we will also uncover the hidden power of vehicle numbers and how having a "lucky" one can influence your journey in more ways than you might imagine.

Question 76: How do mobile numbers play a significant role in Numerology?

Mobile numbers hold importance in Numerology due to the numerological values and energies associated with them. Each number carries its unique vibration that can influence our personal energy field, encompassing our thoughts, actions, and even our environment. In today's world, it is hard to imagine a moment without our cell phones by our side. Not only do we carry the radiation of our phones, but we also carry the vibrations of their numbers.

Mobile phones have evolved into more than just communication tools. They serve as portals to opportunities and even function as our wallets. Hence, it is crucial for the vibration of our mobile numbers to align harmoniously with our own numerological numbers.

By considering the numerological significance of our mobile numbers, we can create a harmonious energetic connection with our devices. This alignment can contribute to a positive and balanced flow of energy in our lives. It is a way to ensure that the energy we surround ourselves with, including our mobile phones, resonates well with our own personal vibration.

Question 77: What is the process of calculating a mobile number in numerology? Should the country code be included when calculating a mobile number in numerology?

To calculate a mobile number in numerology, add up all the individual digits in the number, excluding the country code or area code. The country code is not considered in the calculation as it doesn't directly influence the individual's numerological profile, as it would be common for everyone using a number from that country.

Question 78: What is the significance of house number in Numerology?

House numbers hold importance in Numerology due to the unique energy and vibration associated with each number. Just as numbers influence various aspects of our lives, including our personality and relationships, they can also impact our living spaces. The energy of the surrounding area, including the house number, has the power to influence the occupants.

In addition to considering the principles of Vastu or Feng Shui, it is essential to take into account the numerological compatibility of a house number. By selecting a compatible house number, individuals can enhance their chances of experiencing success, happiness, love, togetherness, and prosperity within their home.

Numerology provides insights into the energetic qualities of different numbers, allowing individuals to make informed decisions about their living spaces. By aligning the vibration of the house number with the energy of the occupants, a harmonious and supportive environment can be created. This alignment contributes to a positive and balanced atmosphere, enhancing the overall well-being and harmony of those residing in the house.

Question 79: What should I do if my house number is not considered lucky in Numerology?

If you find that your house number is not considered lucky according to Numerology, you may wonder if it's necessary to change it. While changing a house can be an option to improve the energy and attract more positive vibrations, it's important to consider various factors before making a decision.

Changing a house can involve practical considerations and potential challenges. It may require updating legal documents, notifying contacts, and financial implications. Therefore, changing a house may not always be a feasible or easy option for everyone.

However, if changing the house is possible and aligns with your personal growth and well-being, it can be a positive step towards creating a more harmonious and numerologically compatible living environment. Embracing change can lead to personal growth, adaptability, and improved well-being.

Before deciding to change the house, there are other ways to enhance the energy within your home. You can make numerological adjustments, consider the principles of Vastu or Feng Shui, add plants or artwork that promote positive energy, and maintain a clean and organised space.

It's important to remember that while numerology can provide insights and guidance, individuals have the freedom to shape their own lives. House number is just one aspect that influences the energy within a home, and you have the ability to create a positive and nurturing environment by implementing various strategies and practices.

Later in the book, I will provide tips on how to work with house numbers to enhance their positive energy and promote a harmonious living space.

Question 80: What is the significance and potential benefits of having a "lucky" vehicle number?

A lucky vehicle number holds significance as it is believed to bring positive energy, good fortune, and protection to the vehicle's owner while driving. It instils confidence, comfort, and a sense of positive vibes during journeys.

The perception of good luck associated with a lucky vehicle number influences the owner's mindset and creates a positive driving experience. It fosters feelings of harmony and being in sync with life's flow.

Additionally, a vehicle with a lucky number may have a higher resale value compared to one with an ordinary or less favourable number. People, often influenced by their beliefs or cultural significance of certain numbers, may be willing to pay a premium for a vehicle with a lucky number.

Question 81: What numerological remedies can be implemented to enhance happiness and satisfaction in a house with the number 22, considering the current inability to change the residence?

In numerology, number 4 (22 so, $2 + 2 = 4$) is connected to building a strong foundation, stability, and practicality. However, it can also have its challenges. Here are some potential challenges associated with the house number 4 from a numerological perspective:

1. **Rigidity and Inflexibility:** Number 4 symbolises stability and practicality. While these traits are beneficial in many aspects, they can lead to rigidity and resistance to change. People residing in a house with number 4 may find it challenging to adapt to new circumstances or embrace spontaneity in their lives.

2. **Overly Focused on Work:** Number 4 is often linked to hard work and productivity. Although this can be advantageous, it may also cause individuals to become overly focused on work, neglecting other essential aspects of life such as family, relationships, and leisure. Striking a balance between work and personal life can be a struggle.

3. **Lack of Creativity and Imagination:** The practical and grounded nature of number 4 may lead to a lack of imagination and creativity. In a house with this number, it is essential to consciously cultivate and express creativity to counterbalance the practical energy.

4. **Tendency Towards Perfectionism:** Number 4 fosters a desire for order and perfection. While striving for excellence can be positive, it may result in excessive perfectionism, self-criticism,

and a fear of making mistakes. Learning to embrace imperfections and finding a healthy balance is crucial.

5. **Resistance to Change:** The stable and grounding energy of number 4 can sometimes translate into resistance to change. Residents of a house with the number 4 may find it challenging to embrace new opportunities or step out of their comfort zones. Recognizing the value of change and adaptability is essential for personal growth and development.

6. **Strained Personal Relationships:** A strong, practical focus of number 4 can sometimes create challenges in personal relationships. It is important for those living in such a house to prioritise quality time with loved ones, and ensure that they are not neglecting their emotional connections.

Here are some remedies that can be considered for challenges associated with the house number 4:

1. **Embrace Flexibility and Change:** Encourage flexibility by engaging in activities or hobbies that break away from rigid routines. Embrace change as a natural part of life and approach it with an open mind.

2. **Balance Work and Personal Life:** Set boundaries between work and personal time. Make time for rest, leisure, hobbies, and creating quality moments with loved ones.

3. **Nurture Creativity:** Engage in creative activities such as painting, writing, or playing a musical instrument. Seek inspiration from art, nature, or diverse cultures to stimulate imagination.

4. **Embrace Imperfections:** Practise self-compassion and self-acceptance. Set attainable goals and celebrate the small victories that you achieve along the way. Understand that perfection is not the ultimate end goal.

5. **Enhance Your Earth Element:** Spend time in nature, gardening, or practise earthing techniques (barefoot walking, outdoor meditation etc) to strengthen your connection with the Earth and promote balance and stability.

6. **Maintain a Clutter-Free Environment:** Keep your house clean and clutter-free to allow energies to move freely and create a harmonious atmosphere.

7. **Consider Wooden Furniture:** Incorporate wooden furniture, which aligns with the Earth element, into your home to further enhance the positive aspects of number 4.

8. **Avoid Faulty Electronics:** Ensure faulty electronic devices are repaired or replaced. Displaying malfunctioning electronics can disrupt energy flow in the house.

9. **Maintain Iron Grills and Doors:** Keep a check on rusting iron grills or doors and maintain them properly. This supports the stability associated with the number 4.

10. **Name Your House:** Instead of simply writing "22" on the nameplate, consider adding "HOUSE NO. 22" to strengthen the significance of the number and create a positive, stable identity for your home.

CHAPTER 11

NUMEROLOGY AND CAREER PATHWAYS: NAVIGATING PROFESSIONAL SUCCESS

In this chapter, we will explore how numerology can serve as a compass in helping you navigate the professional realm.

Discover the fascinating connection between the elements in numerology and common career themes. Unearth how understanding these elemental influences can assist you in identifying potential career paths that resonate with your innate strengths and passions.

But that's not all – in this chapter, we will also uncover the intriguing correlation between specific birth numbers in numerology and potential vocations or career paths.

Question 82: Can numerology guide me in my career choices?

Numerology can indeed guide you in making career choices by offering valuable insights and guidance. Here's how numerology can help:

1. **Birth Number and Destiny Number:** Your birth number and destiny number in numerology represents the core purpose and direction of your life. They provide insight into the types of careers and paths that may align with your natural talents, abilities, and passions. For example, if your birth number is 1 which is associated with leadership and individuality, you might thrive in careers that allow you to take charge or work independently.

2. **Exploration of Interests and Passions:** Numerology can help you uncover your personal interests and passions by examining the numbers associated with your hobbies, likes, and dislikes. By aligning your career choices with your genuine interests and passions, you increase the likelihood of finding fulfilment and success in your chosen path.

3. **Personal Year:** Numerology considers the current year you're in, known as your Personal Year. Each Personal Year has its own unique energy and themes. Understanding the influence of your Personal Year can help you make career decisions at the right time or navigate through periods of change or opportunity.

4. **Integration with Other Factors:** While numerology provides valuable insights, it's important to consider it in conjunction with other factors. Self-reflection, research, considering your skills, experiences, talents, education, seeking professional guidance, and putting in hard work are all essential components of making informed career decisions.

By combining the wisdom of numerology with self-reflection and practical considerations, you can make better, informed career choices that align with your unique numerical influences.

Question 83: What are some common career themes associated with the elements in numerology, and how can understanding these elemental influences help individuals in identifying potential career paths that align with their natural strengths and inclinations?

In numerology, the elements associated with zodiac signs can offer valuable insights into potential career paths that align with an individual's natural strengths and inclinations. By understanding these elemental influences, individuals can discover professions that bring them fulfilment and success.

1. **Fire Signs (Aries, Leo, Sagittarius)**

   Fire signs are driven by passion, creativity, and leadership qualities. They thrive in dynamic environments and enjoy taking charge. Potential careers may include entrepreneurship, sales, marketing, entertainment, sports, motivational speaking, or any field that requires enthusiasm and initiative.

2. **Earth Signs (Taurus, Virgo, Capricorn)**

   Earth signs are practical, reliable, and detail-oriented. They excel in roles that demand organisation and problem-solving. Potential careers may include finance, accounting, project management, architecture, engineering, real estate, agriculture, or any field that values stability and a methodical approach.

3. **Air Signs (Gemini, Libra, Aquarius)**

   Air signs flourish in careers that utilise their intellect, communication skills, and social acumen. They excel in networking, research, analysis, and strategic thinking. Potential careers may include writing, journalism, teaching, counselling, social media management, event planning, or any field that involves engaging with ideas and people.

4. Water Signs (Cancer, Scorpio, Pisces)

> Water signs possess emotional depth, intuition, and empathy. They excel in careers involving emotional connection and creativity. Potential paths may include psychology, counselling, healing arts, social work, art, music, writing, acting, or any field that taps into their understanding of human emotions.

Question 84: What are some potential vocations or career paths that are commonly associated with specific birth numbers in numerology?

In numerology, each birth number is associated with specific qualities and vibrations that can shape an individual's vocational interests. While personal circumstances and other factors should also be considered, here are some potential vocations commonly linked to specific birth numbers:

1. **Birth Number 1:** Leadership roles, entrepreneurship, executive positions, creative fields, self-employment, motivational speaker, sales, marketing, public relations.

2. **Birth Number 2:** Counselling, psychology, social work, diplomacy, mediation, teaching, writing, customer service, teamwork-oriented roles, healthcare, event planning.

3. **Birth Number 3:** Performing arts, writing, journalism, communication, public speaking, teaching, advertising, marketing, social media, creative fields, entertainment.

4. **Birth Number 4:** Engineering, architecture, project management, accounting, finance, administration, organisation, logistics, craftsmanship, research, real estate.

5. **Birth Number 5:** Travel and tourism, sales, marketing, public relations, media, communication, journalism, politics, entrepreneurship, freelance work, event planning.

6. **Birth Number 6:** Healthcare, counselling, teaching, social work, human resources, hospitality, interior design, fashion, media, creative fields, parenting, coaching, community service.

7. **Birth Number 7:** Research, analysis, psychology, counselling, spirituality, philosophy, writing, teaching, academia, scientific fields, investigative work.

8. **Birth Number 8:** Business, finance, entrepreneurship, leadership roles, management, real estate, investments, law, executive positions in the corporate sector.

9. **Birth Number 9:** Humanitarian work, counselling, therapy, social activism, teaching, writing, artistry, spirituality, healing professions, philanthropy, armed forces.

CHAPTER 12

CHROMATIC VIBRATIONS: EXPLORING NUMEROLOGY'S CONNECTION WITH COLOURS AND GEMSTONES

This chapter delves into the fascinating realm of how colours influence our personal vibrations and how gemstones are believed to hold the power of remedies and enhancements in numerology.

Discover the secrets of lucky colours that align with specific birth numbers, infusing life with positive energies and good fortune. Unearth the gemstones commonly associated with uplifting an individual's spirit and creating a harmonious aura around them.

But there's more to the story. Ever wondered why black is often avoided on important occasions? We will unravel the reasons behind this practice and the significance of the traditional "kala tika" or black mark on a baby's forehead.

Question 85: How do colours correspond to numerology and impact our personal vibrations?

Colours play a significant role in numerology as they possess their own distinct vibrations and meanings. These colours have the power to interact with our energy fields and influence our emotions, thoughts, and overall well-being. By understanding the relationship between numerology and colours, we can harness their energy to align with our life's purpose and enhance our personal vibrations.

In numerology, each number is associated with specific vibrational qualities and symbolism. Similarly, colours resonate with particular frequencies that can affect us on a profound level. By recognizing the numerological significance of colours, we can leverage their energy to harmonise with our unique traits and amplify positive attributes.

For instance, let's consider birth number 9, which embodies passion, energy, and vitality. This number is ruled by Mars, the fiery planet. In numerology, the colour red is often associated with these characteristics as it represents passion, vitality, and strength. By incorporating red into their environment, clothing, or accessories, individuals with birth number 9 can enhance their innate qualities and boost their self-confidence.

Similarly, other birth numbers may resonate with different colours based on their distinct traits. By understanding these correspondences, we can consciously select colours that align with our numerological vibrations, promoting a sense of balance, well-being, and personal growth.

The significance of colours in numerology lies in their ability to enhance and harmonise with our personal vibrations. By intentionally incorporating specific colours into our lives, we can create environments that resonate with our numerological traits, supporting our journey towards self-realisation and fulfilment.

Ultimately, understanding how colours correspond to numerology empowers us to create a more harmonious and meaningful existence. By embracing colours that align with our numerological vibrations, we can infuse our lives with positive energy, heightened awareness, and a deeper connection to our authentic selves.

Question 86: What are the lucky colours associated with specific birth numbers in numerology?

In numerology, each birth number is believed to have lucky colours associated with it, which can bring positive energies and enhance various aspects of life. While individual interpretations may vary, here are some commonly associated lucky colours for each birth number:

1. **Birth Number 1:** Gold, orange, yellow, white, and bronze are lucky colours that represent energy, leadership, and ambition. These colours can boost confidence and attract success.

2. **Birth Number 2:** Pale blue, white, cream, and silver are considered lucky colours, symbolising harmony, balance, and diplomacy. These colours can foster peace and encourage cooperation.

3. **Birth Number 3:** Yellow, lemon, violet, purple, and bright shades are lucky colours that evoke creativity, joy, and self-expression. These colours can bring inspiration and a positive outlook.

4. **Birth Number 4:** Yellow, orange, blue, and earthy brown tones are lucky colours that signify stability, grounding, and practicality. They provide a sense of security and reliability.

5. **Birth Number 5:** White, green, silver, blue, and aquamarine are lucky colours associated with freedom, adventure, and versatility. These colours can ignite enthusiasm and adaptability.

6. **Birth Number 6:** Pink, peach, blue, and soft pastels are lucky colours embodying love, nurturing, and harmony. They promote compassion and create a calming atmosphere.

7. **Birth Number 7:** Green, white, blue, and cream are lucky colours representing spirituality, intuition, and wisdom. These colours can enhance inner reflection and insight.

8. **Birth Number 8:** Light blue, yellow, cream, white, and light grey are considered lucky colours that evoke a sense of strength and prosperity.

9. **Birth Number 9:** Maroon, crimson, and rich shades are lucky colours symbolising compassion, spirituality, and transformation. These colours inspire deep emotional connections and empathy.

Question 87: How do gemstones relate to numerology in terms of prescribing remedies or enhancing outcomes?

Gemstones do have a role in numerology when it comes to prescribing remedies or enhancing outcomes. According to numerology beliefs, specific gemstones are associated with particular numbers and are thought to possess metaphysical properties that can influence our lives.

Each number in numerology is believed to have its own characteristics and energies. Gemstones that align with these energies are considered beneficial for individuals associated with those numbers. For instance, if someone has a birth number 7, they may be advised to wear a cat's eye gemstone. Cat's eye is believed to help ward off sudden misfortune and alleviate feelings of depression, which are challenges associated with the number 7.

Wearing or using gemstones associated with one's numerological number is believed to enhance the positive qualities linked to that number and provide support in overcoming its associated challenges. It is important to note that the effectiveness of gemstones in numerology can vary depending on personal beliefs and individual experiences.

Question 88: What gemstones are commonly believed to bring positivity and uplift the energy around an individual?

There are several gemstones commonly believed to bring positivity and uplift the energy around an individual. Here are a couple of them:

1. **Citrine:** Often referred to as the "Stone of Abundance," citrine is associated with joy, abundance, and positive energy. It is believed to attract prosperity, enhance self-confidence, and foster a positive outlook on life.

2. **Amethyst:** Known for its calming and spiritual properties, amethyst is considered to be the stone of positivity. It is believed to promote inner peace, aid in spiritual growth, and help develop a positive mindset.

Both citrine and amethyst are treasured for their ability to create a positive and harmonious atmosphere. Whether worn as jewellery, kept in the living space, or used during meditation, these gemstones are believed to radiate positive energies and bring beneficial effects to those who embrace their qualities.

Question 89: What are the reasons behind the practice of avoiding the colour black on important occasions?

The avoidance of the colour black on important occasions is rooted in cultural beliefs and symbolism. Black is often associated with mourning, grief, or negative emotions. It is considered a colour of sadness and sorrow, which is why people tend to avoid wearing black during joyous or celebratory events.

In some cultures, black is linked to death and is worn as a symbol of mourning. Using black prominently on happy occasions might be seen as inappropriate or inauspicious. Instead, people prefer to wear vibrant and colourful attire during festivities to create a lively and cheerful atmosphere.

Additionally, there are beliefs that black absorbs energy, including negative energy. Wearing black during positive occasions may be thought to attract or absorb negativity, potentially affecting one's mood or well-being. To maintain a positive and joyful ambiance during important events, people choose to avoid black colour.

Question 90: Why is it common to put a black mark or a "kala tika" on a baby's forehead if wearing black is considered inauspicious in some contexts?

The black mark or "kala tika" on a baby's forehead is believed to have protective properties. Although wearing black attire may be considered inauspicious in certain contexts due to its association with negativity, the "kala tika" is viewed differently. It is believed that the black mark can ward off or absorb negative energies, acting as a shield to protect the baby from potential harm or evil influences. The "kala tika" is a symbol of safeguarding the child's well-being and is commonly used in many cultures as a traditional practice.

CHAPTER 13

THE ART OF SIGNATURES: CRAFTING AN AUSPICIOUS IMPRESSION

In this chapter, we will unravel the importance of signatures in the world of numerology and how they can significantly impact our lives.

Find out the numerological significance of cutting your name with a backstroke in your signature. What does it reveal about your unique vibrations and energy?

Also, discover valuable advice on how to create an auspicious signature that resonates harmoniously with your personal vibrations, promoting positivity and success.

Question 91: What is the importance of signature in Numerology? How does it affect our lives?

The signature holds importance in numerology as it represents a personalised vibration and reflects our unique identity. It affects our lives by influencing the energy we project and the experiences we attract. By consciously shaping our signature, we can align our energy, enhance self-expression, and potentially attract positive experiences in our lives.

Here are a few reasons why signature holds importance in numerology:

1. **Personal vibration:** Each letter in our signature is associated with a specific numerical value in numerology. By analysing the numerical values of the letters in our signature, we can gain insights into our personality traits, strengths, and challenges. This knowledge can help us understand ourselves better and make conscious choices aligned with our authentic selves.

2. **Self-expression and identity:** Our signature is more than just a scribble; it is a representation of our identity and how we choose to present ourselves to the world. It reflects our individuality, creativity, and personal style. By consciously shaping our signature, we can express ourselves authentically and communicate our unique energy to others.

3. **Energetic resonance:** Each letter in our signature carries its own energetic vibration. When combined, these vibrations create a unique energy pattern. This pattern interacts with the vibrations of the universe and can influence the experiences and opportunities that come our way. By aligning our signature with our desired outcomes and intentions, we can enhance our energetic resonance and attract positive experiences into our lives.

4. **Signature analysis:** Numerologists analyse signatures to gain deeper insights into a person's characteristics, aspirations, and potential. They examine factors such as the shape of the letters, the flow of the signature, the size, and other elements to decipher the underlying energy and symbolism. This analysis provides valuable guidance and suggestions for aligning the signature with an individual's desired goals or personal development.

Question 92: What is the numerological significance of cutting my name with a backstroke in my signature?

The numerological significance of cutting your name with a backstroke in your signature depends on the specific numbers and vibrations associated with your name. Numerology assigns numerical values to letters and analyses their influence on one's personality and life journey. However, in general, cutting a name with a backstroke, can have symbolic meanings.

1. **Need to establish identity:** When your name is cut with a backstroke, it might indicate a strong need to establish your own identity and make your presence known. It reflects a sense of self-assuredness and a willingness to stand up for your beliefs and values.

2. **Desire for self-reflection:** The backstroke cutting through your name may also suggest a desire for self-reflection and introspection. It shows that you are willing to examine your own identity, choices, and actions, seeking deeper understanding and self-awareness.

3. **Yearning for freedom:** Cutting your name with a backstroke can symbolise a yearning for freedom and a desire to break free from perceived limitations or constraints. It showcases your courage to challenge societal norms or expectations, and a willingness to embrace individuality.

4. **Expression of discontent:** For some individuals, the backstroke through their name might indicate a sense of discontent or dissatisfaction with their existence. It could be a reflection of regressive thinking, stress, or even depression that needs attention and resolution.

Question 93: What numerological advice can you provide to create an auspicious signature that aligns harmoniously with my personal vibrations and promotes positive energy?

Creating an auspicious signature is a wonderful way to align with the positive energies of numerology and make a unique mark that represents your true self. Here are some numerological tips to help you design a harmonious signature:

1. **Numerological alignment:** Begin by understanding the numerical vibrations of your birth name. Each letter in your name carries a specific numerical value, which has its own significance and influence. Study the numerology of your name and seek to incorporate letters and their corresponding numbers that resonate positively with your birth date's numerology. This alignment will create a harmonious connection between your name and signature.

2. **Balance and flow:** Aim for a balanced signature that maintains a sense of symmetry and flow. Avoid excessive variations in letter sizes, slants, or spacing, as they can disrupt the overall harmony of your signature. A balanced signature reflects stability and coherence, symbolising your ability to handle situations with grace and composure.

3. **Legibility and clarity:** While designing your signature, make sure it remains clear and legible. A messy or illegible signature might create confusion and misunderstandings. A clear and distinct signature contributes to effective communication and conveys a sense of professionalism and confidence.

4. **Upward slant:** Consider writing your signature with a slight upward slant, at around a 45-degree angle. This upward direction represents growth, progress, and a positive outlook. It suggests an upward trajectory in life, striving towards higher goals, and a forward-moving mindset. This slant may reflect a sense of optimism and determination, empowering you to overcome challenges and embrace opportunities.

5. **Authenticity:** While incorporating numerological principles into your signature, ensure that the changes you make align with your authentic self. Your signature should be a genuine representation of who you are and what you aspire to be. Embrace the positive aspects of numerology while staying true to your personality and identity.

CHAPTER 14

THE MAGIC SQUARE: DECODING NUMEROLOGICAL SECRETS IN THE LO SHU GRID

In this chapter, we will get into the realm of the Lo Shu Grid, exploring its significance and symbolism, learning about the horizontal and vertical planes that form the foundation of this magical square, each carrying unique meanings and interpretations.

Discover the intriguing aspects of the mental, emotional, and practical planes within the Lo Shu Grid, and how they influence the course of our lives. Also, unravel the secrets of the Thought, Will, and Action planes, and how their alignment can bring harmony and balance to our existence.

And not only this, you will also learn how to make your own Lo Shu grid.

Question 94: What is Lo Shu Grid in numerology?

The Lo Shu Grid, also known as the Lo Shu Square, is a 3x3 grid that holds profound significance in Chinese numerology. Legend has it that this grid was discovered on the back of a mystical turtle that emerged from the Yellow River over 4,000 years ago. It is revered as a representation of the balance and harmony of the universe, making it an essential tool in various divination practices, including Feng Shui, Chinese astrology, and numerology.

Within the Lo Shu Grid, each square contains a specific number arranged in a particular pattern. Remarkably, the numbers in each row, column, and diagonal of the grid all add up to the same total, which is 15. This arrangement of numbers carries deep symbolic meaning, reflecting the equilibrium of the five elements (wood, fire, earth, metal, and water) and other cosmic forces.

The Lo Shu Grid serves as a powerful instrument for divination. Its patterns and relationships provide insights into different facets of life, including health, relationships, career, and more. For example, a practitioner may ask a question and then use the Lo Shu Grid to determine the answer based on the patterns and relationships of the numbers in the grid, where:

- Number 1 signifies career and communication.

- Number 2 signifies marriage and relationships.

- Number 3 signifies health and education.

- Number 4 signifies discipline and money.

- Number 5 signifies stability and balance.

- Number 6 signifies friends and luxury.

- Number 7 signifies creativity and children.

- Number 8 signifies knowledge and wealth.

- Number 9 signifies fame and energy.

Question 95: What are horizontal and vertical planes of Lo Shu Grid?

In the Lo Shu grid, the arrangement of numbers forms a 3x3 square, and it can be divided into both horizontal and vertical planes. The horizontal plane consists of the following three rows:

- **Mental Plane (1st Row):** The first row of the grid contains the numbers 4, 9, and 2.

- **Emotional Plane (2nd Row):** The second row consists of the numbers 3, 5, and 7.

- **Practical Plane (3rd Row):** The third row contains the numbers 8, 1, and 6.

The vertical planes are formed by the following three columns of numbers:

- **Thought Plane (1st Column):** The first column includes the numbers 4, 3, and 8.

- **Will Plane (2nd Column):** The second column contains the numbers 9, 5, and 1.

- **Action Plane (3rd Column):** The third column consists of the numbers 2, 7, and 6.

Question 96: What are the meanings and interpretations of the Mental, Emotional, and Practical planes in the Lo Shu grid?

In the Lo Shu grid, each row represents a different aspect of a person's life. Let's understand the meanings and interpretations of the mental, emotional, and practical planes:

1. **Mental Plane:** This plane is associated with the first column of the Lo Shu grid. It gives insights into a person's mental abilities and intellectual prowess. The numbers in this column reveal

how well someone can analyse information, think critically, and process thoughts. A strong mental plane suggests sharp thinking and problem-solving skills, while a weak one may indicate the need for improvement in cognitive abilities.

2. **Emotional Plane:** The second column of the Lo Shu grid represents the emotional plane. It sheds light on a person's emotional nature and sensitivity. The numbers in this column reflect how individuals handle their feelings, empathy towards others, and emotional well-being. A balanced emotional plane indicates emotional intelligence and healthy emotional responses, while an imbalanced one may suggest emotional challenges that need attention.

3. **Practical Plane:** Associated with the third column, the practical plane is all about the physical aspects of life. It reflects a person's practical skills, ability to manifest goals, and their relationship with material resources. A strong practical plane signifies resourcefulness, groundedness, and efficiency in managing real-world matters. On the other hand, a weak practical plane may indicate the need for better practical decision-making and resource management.

Question 97: What are the meanings and interpretations of the Thought plane, Will plane, and Action plane in the Lo Shu grid?

In the Lo Shu grid, each column also represents a different aspect of our being. Let's explore the meanings and interpretations of the Thought plane, Will plane, and Action planes:

1. **Thought Plane:** The Thought plane is all about our mental faculties and intellectual abilities. It encompasses our thoughts, ideas, and capacity for analysis. This plane is associated with intelligence, creativity, and our ability to come up with innovative solutions to problems. A strong Thought plane suggests a sharp and imaginative mind, while a weaker one may indicate the need to enhance logical thinking and problem-solving skills.

2. **Will Plane:** The Will plane reflects our inner drive and motivation. It represents our desires, ambitions, and willpower to pursue our goals. This plane governs our ability to make decisions and take action to achieve what we desire. Traits like persistence, determination, and assertiveness are linked to a strong Will plane. A balanced Will plane indicates the ability to overcome obstacles and stay focused on our aspirations.

3. **Action Plane:** The Action plane is all about practicality and productivity. It represents our ability to turn our thoughts and desires into tangible results through physical actions. This plane is closely related to our work ethic, efficiency, and diligence. A strong Action plane suggests good organisational skills and the capability to execute plans effectively. On the other hand, a weak Action plane may indicate the need for better time management and practical problem-solving abilities.

Question 98: Can you please provide step-by-step instructions on how to create a Lo Shu grid, including the placement of numbers and the specific pattern to follow?

To create a Lo Shu grid, follow these steps:

1. Start with a square grid that consists of nine squares arranged in a 3x3 pattern.

2. In the centre square of the grid, write the number 5. This square represents the number 5 which is considered to be the centre of the Lo Shu grid.

3. Proceed to fill in the remaining squares of the grid with the numbers 1 to 9, following a specific pattern.

4	9	2
3	5	7
8	1	6

4. Once you have filled in all the numbers, your grid is complete.
   The resulting grid should display a 3x3 square with the
   numbers arranged as shown above.

The completed grid is known as the Lo Shu grid, and it is the basis
for the Lo Shu Square.

Question 99: How can I create a Lo Shu grid based on my birthdate, which is 26th March 1975?

1. Start with a blank 3x3 grid:

2. Assign each square in the grid a number from 1 to 9, starting
   from the top-left square and moving from left to right and top
   to bottom.

3. According to the traditional Chinese Lo Shu grid, the numbers
   are placed in a specific pattern. Starting from the centre square,
   follow the pattern of placing the numbers in a counter-
   clockwise spiral:

4	9	2
3	5	7
8	1	6

4. Take the digits of the birth year (1975) and write them down: 1,
   9, 7, and 5.

5. Place these digits in the respective squares of the grid:

	9	
	5	7
	1	

6. Take the month of birth (March), which corresponds to number 3.

7. Place the number 3 in the remaining empty square:

	9	
3	5	7
	1	

8. Finally, take the day of birth (26) and place the digits 2 and 6 in the remaining empty squares:

	9	2
3	5	7
	1	6

9. Now take the total of your birth number i.e. 2+6 = 8 and Destiny number i.e.

$$2+6+3+1+9+7+5 = 33, 3+3 = 6$$

	9	2
3	5	7
8	1	6 6

10. Once you have filled in all the numbers, your Chinese Lo Shu grid based on the birth date 26th March 1975 is complete.

CHAPTER 15

LAUGHING WITH NUMBERS: FUN AND QUIRKY QUESTIONS IN NUMEROLOGY

Now that we've delved into the depths of numerology, let's lighten the mood and explore some fun and light-hearted questions! Get ready for a playful twist on numerology as we dive into the world of humorous inquiries. Are you ready to laugh and have some fun with numerology?

Let's embark on a joyous journey through amusing numerological questions before you finish reading this book!

Question 100: If numbers went on a vacation, where would they go and why?

If numbers took a vacation, they would each have their unique preferences based on their traits and characteristics:

1. **Number 1:** This number is all about independence and ambition. So, it might choose to go on a solo trip to a serene mountain retreat. It would seek some quiet time away from the

hustle and bustle of life, using the vacation as an opportunity for self-reflection and personal growth.

2. **Number 2:** The number 2 is all about cooperation and harmony. For its vacation, it would probably opt for a peaceful beachside getaway. The calming sound of ocean waves would soothe its soul, and it would enjoy spending quality time with friends and loved ones, nurturing those close relationships.

3. **Number 3:** Known for its creativity and expressiveness, number 3 would love to visit a vibrant city with a rich cultural scene. It would immerse itself in art, music, and entertainment, revelling in the creative energy of the place.

4. **Number 4:** Practical and structured, number 4 would prefer a well-organised tour to historical landmarks and architectural wonders. It would appreciate the significance of heritage and tradition, making the most of its vacation by learning about the past.

5. **Number 5:** With its adventurous and spontaneous nature, number 5 would undoubtedly choose a backpacking trip across different countries. It craves excitement, new experiences, and cultural diversity, and a globetrotting adventure would be perfect for it.

6. **Number 6:** The number 6 is all about family and nurturing. So, it would opt for a family vacation to a cosy countryside retreat. The focus would be on spending quality time together and connecting with nature.

7. **Number 7:** This number seeks knowledge and introspection. It might choose to visit a serene meditation retreat or a secluded library, diving into books and expanding its wisdom during the vacation.

8. **Number 8:** Ambitious and success-driven, number 8 would pick a luxurious destination with high-end resorts. It would indulge in lavish experiences and perhaps use the vacation as an opportunity for networking and business opportunities.

9. **Number 9:** The compassionate and philanthropic number 9 would likely decide to spend its vacation volunteering in a developing country. Engaging in humanitarian efforts and making a positive impact would be its way of giving back to the world.

Question 101: If numbers could talk, which one would have the best sense of humour?

If numbers had the gift of speech, number 5 would undoubtedly be the one with the best sense of humour. This fun-loving and adventurous number has a natural ability to find humour in all sorts of situations. Whether it's cracking witty jokes or making clever remarks, number 5 would keep everyone entertained with its playful personality. It loves excitement and laughter, and its charismatic nature would effortlessly bring a smile to people's faces. So, in the world of talking numbers, number 5 would be the life of the party, spreading joy and laughter wherever it goes.

Question 102: If numbers could throw a party, which one would be the life of the party?

If numbers were to host a party, number 3 and number 6 would undoubtedly be the life of the party. These numbers are known for their vibrant and social personalities, always seeking to bring joy and entertainment to others. With their creativity and expressive nature, they would go all out to create an exciting and memorable event. Laughter, music, and a lively atmosphere would fill the party, thanks to their infectious energy. Their natural charm and ability to connect with people would ensure that everyone feels welcome and included, making the party an absolute blast. So, if you ever receive an invitation to a party hosted by number 3 and number 6, you can expect a fantastic time and unforgettable memories.

Question 103: If numbers had personalities, which one would be the most mysterious?

If numbers had personalities, number 7 would likely be the most mysterious one. In numerology, number 7 is often associated with mystery, spirituality, and introspection. It is considered a deeply ruminative and analytical number that seeks to uncover hidden truths and delve into the unknown. Number 7's mysterious nature would add an element of intrigue and curiosity to any situation, keeping everyone on their toes and guessing what number 7 is thinking of. So, if you ever encounter a mystifying and enigmatic presence, there's a good chance it's the secretive number 7 at work.

Question 104: If numbers could choose their dream vacation destination, where would number 2 go and why?

If numbers could pick their dream vacation spot, number 2 would likely go to a serene and picturesque place like the Maldives or Goa. Being harmonious and appreciative of natural beauty, number 2 would relish the tranquil beaches, clear waters, and the chance to unwind and immerse itself in nature's wonders. These locations would perfectly align with the peaceful and balanced nature of number 2, making it the ideal dream vacation destination.

Question 105: What are some appropriate and representative hashtags for each number that capture their unique qualities and characteristics?

1. **Number 1:** #NumberOneGoals #FirstPlace #LeadingThePack

2. **Number 2:** #TwosCompany #DynamicDuo #PartnersInCrime

3. **Number 3:** #CreativeExpressions #ArtisticVibes #ThreesACharm

4. **Number 4:** #OrganizedLife #SteadyAndStructured #FourOnTheFloor

5. **Number 5:** #Wanderlust #AdventurousSoul #LiveLifeToTheFullest

6. **Number 6:** #FamilyTime #HomeSweetHome #SixSenses

7. **Number 7:** #DeepThoughts #LuckyNumberSeven #MysticalMind

8. **Number 8:** #SuccessStory #AmbitiousGoals #FinancialFreedom

9. **Number 9:** #KindnessMatters #GenerousSpirit #NineWithHeart

EPILOGUE

As I embarked on the journey of writing this book, my initial intention was to explore the realm of numerology through the lens of 105 questions. Little did I know that the world of numbers would seize my imagination, filling my mind with a seemingly endless stream of inquiries, answers, and inspiration. The more I delved into the depths of this captivating subject, the more it beckoned me to dive even deeper and weave another tapestry of knowledge in the form of a new book.

Yet, as I reflect upon the pages before me, I find solace in knowing that this collection of questions and answers has the power to satisfy the inquisitive minds that seek understanding. It is my sincerest hope that within these chapters, a wealth of numerological wisdom has found its way into the hearts and minds of those who have ventured alongside me.

Through our shared journey, I trust that you, too, have been enriched by the beauty and intricacy of this ancient science. The exploration of numerology is like a voyage of self-discovery, unlocking hidden truths and illuminating the profound connection between numbers and our existence. As we traversed this path together, I hope that each turn of the page brought new-found insights, a deeper appreciation for the significance of numbers, and a sense of wonder at the intricate tapestry that underlies our universe.

While the prospect of another book beckons, let us take a moment to relish the fulfilment that this current endeavour has brought. The satisfaction of exploring 105 questions, unearthing their answers, and sharing the knowledge gained is a testament to our collective pursuit of wisdom.

Thank you for joining me on this extraordinary journey through the realms of numerology. May the wisdom gained within these pages continue to inspire and illuminate your path, serving as a guiding light on your personal quest for understanding and self-discovery.

ACKNOWLEDGEMENTS

I would like to take a moment to express my deepest gratitude to the individuals who have played a pivotal role in the creation of this numerology book. Their unwavering support, encouragement, and belief in me have been the driving force behind its completion.

First and foremost, I want to extend my heartfelt appreciation to my beloved husband, Anjani B Kuumar. Your love, constant championing, and support have been the foundation upon which this book was built. Your role as my life partner goes beyond words, as you have also been my mentor and guide, inspiring me to push boundaries and believe in my abilities to achieve more. Your endless faith in my work has been the fuel that propelled me forward.

To my darling daughter, Jahnvvi Kuumar, I adore you and your ability to always show me new perspectives. As an accomplished author yourself, your positive and thoughtful insights have been invaluable throughout this journey. Your confidence in me has served as a ceaseless source of purpose. Thank you for having my back as I explore new horizons, and for being my biggest cheerleader.

My sincerest appreciation to my brother, Braj Raj, whose pride in my success instils drive and motivation in me. Your perpetual support and credence in my abilities has given me the conviction to pursue my passions. Thank you for always being in my corner and encouraging me to reach for the stars.

To my mother, words cannot express the depth of my gratitude for your affirmations and assurances since day one. Thank you for making me believe that I can achieve anything I set my mind to. Your boundless faith in me has been a guiding light, and I am forever appreciative of your presence in my life.

I would also like to pay tribute to my late father, who must be watching over me from among the stars. Your love and blessings continue to inspire and guide me. Your memory lives on in my heart, and I dedicate this book to you.

Lastly, I want to add how grateful I am to my clients, Instagram followers, and YouTube subscribers all over the world. You have become an extended family to me, and this book is my gift to you in return for the love, respect, and belief you have always shown in me. Your support and encouragement has been the impetus behind my work and makes it that much more rewarding. I am honoured to have you as part of this incredible journey.

What Next?

1. Learn from Me (FREE)

I keep sharing my knowledge through my YouTube channel on regular basis. There is a vast repository of knowledge already available on my channel (few hundreds of videos/shorts) and lakhs of people all over the world keep watching my videos on regular basis to learn about Numerology and how they can make their life better by using its principles. Do SUBSCRIBE to my YouTube channel (details given below) to be a part of my community and directly learn from me.

www.youtube.com/priyankakuumar

2. Learn while having some Fun (FREE)

I also share my knowledge through Instagram Reels and sometimes interact live with all my followers. In addition, they also get an opportunity to get a peek into my life (sometimes with a funny twist). I am also active on Twitter and Facebook. You can join me on these platforms and start learning while having some fun.

www.instagram.com/priyankakuumar

www.facebook.com/Numberwrksbypriyankakuumar

www.twitter.com/priyanka501

3. Get Your Numerology Report prepared by Me (PAID)

Media calls me the 'Numerologist for the Masses' because I want everyone to get benefitted by using the principles of numerology. I charge a very small fee (probably one-third or one-fourth of what other leading numerologists charge) and prepare a personalised Numerology Report for people who want my help to improve their lives through Numerology. I don't do it free because then, people don't take the report seriously. The report covers the following aspects:

- A detailed understanding of your Personality, what would work for you and what you should be careful about.

- How is your Name affecting your life and Name Correction, if needed.

- Lucky Days and Numbers on which you should carry out your important activities.

- Lucky Colours and Gemstones for you.

- Recommendations for your Mobile Phone Number and House Number.

- Signature Analysis and Correction, if needed.

- Choice of favourable Career options.

- One Business Name Check and Correction, if needed.

If you want my help in getting your Numerology Prepared, you can use any of the following methods:

Visit www.numberwrks.com and Order Your Report online.

Send a WhatsApp message on +91-7506124710 and my team will help you in Ordering Your Numerology Report.

Send a mail to numberwrks@gmail.com and my team will assist you with all the details.